edexcel

ng lives

CW00919569

Literacy

Teacher's Handbook

Level 1

Emma Lee

Consultants **Geoff Barton and Muriel Lloyd Lavery**

A PEARSON COMPANY

Published by:
Edexcel Limited
One90 High Holborn
London
WC1V 7BH
www.edexcel.org.uk

Distributed by:
Pearson Education Limited
Edinburgh Gate
Harlow
Essex
CM20 2JE
www.longman.co.uk

© Edexcel Limited 2006

All rights reserved. No part of this publication may be reproduced, stored in a retrieval system, or transmitted in any form or by any means, electronic, mechanic, photocopying, recording, or otherwise without either the prior permission of the Publishers or a licence permitting restricted copying in the United Kingdom issued by the Copyright Licensing Agency Ltd. 90 Tottenham Court Road, London W1P 9HE.

First published 2006
Fourth impression 2008
ISBN 978-1-84690-137-9

Edited and typeset by Ken Vail Graphic Design
Cover and text design by Ken Vail Graphic Design
Cover image © Image Source/Alamy
Printed and bound in Great Britain at 4edge Limited, Hockley

The publisher's policy is to use paper manufactured from sustainable forests.

Practice Tests CD
This CD was produced as part of the DfES Move On project 2003–6 and carries Crown copyright. Details of the Move On project and its successor Move On Up, commissioned by QIA, can be found at www.move-on.org.uk.

Acknowledgements
The Publisher would like to thank all schools involved in research into this book.

Illustrations by Beehive Illustration (Mark Turner)

The Publisher is grateful to all the copyright owners whose material appears in this book. Every effort has been made to trace the copyright holders and we apologise in advance for any unintentional omissions. We would be pleased to insert the appropriate acknowledgement in any subsequent edition of this publication.

Contents

Introduction: getting the best from Adult Literacy and Adult Numeracy

The Adult Literacy Level 1 Skills Book and Teacher's Handbook

This Teacher's Handbook and accompanying Skills Book have been designed to provide everything you need to teach Level 1 Adult Literacy successfully – whether you are an experienced practitioner or are embarking on the teaching of literacy for the first time.

The materials provided in the Skills Book and the Teacher's Handbook are designed to be **flexible**, suitable for teaching an individual, a group or the whole class. Although written primarily with schools in mind, these books are equally valuable in a college or work-based setting.

The primary purpose of these books is to make the teaching and learning process **as easy and as effective as possible.** To this end, all the skills required to meet the demands of the test have been carefully explained in a way that is understandable to a young person, with exercises specifically devised to reflect what the test requires.

There is freedom for you to cover the sections of the book in the order that suits your students, and you can concentrate on their identified areas of weakness using the **wide range of exercises and test materials** provided, including the Practice Tests CD-ROM provided with this Teacher's Handbook, and the Hot Topics CD-ROM included with the Skills Book, which gives motivating games and activities to help students enjoy practising essential skills.

Each section of the Handbook has **two pages of guidance** on how to teach the skills required. Based on the tried and tested ideas of experienced teachers, these pages will help you teach effectively and in a lively and meaningful way.

To help students gain confidence as they master the skills and to give students more practice before moving on, **six pages of photocopiable material per section** reinforce initial learning by providing exercises similar to those they have already encountered in their Skills Book. This allows for flexibility in teaching, meeting the needs of individuals as well as entire classes.

Progress is easily monitored on the **tracking grid** provided and a **certificate** is included to record the completion of the course. **Answers to all questions are included**, along with further practice suggestions if students have struggled with particular types of question. A further **nine sample tests** are included on the accompanying Practice Tests CD-ROM for additional testing, and this can be used both for revision and practice, and to get students used to doing the tests on computer.

The response of both students and teachers in pre-publication trials has been entirely positive. We hope you enjoy using the materials, and wish you and your students every success!

The Adult Literacy and Adult Numeracy qualifications

The Level 1 Literacy qualification is one of four Adult Literacy and Adult Numeracy qualifications:

- Adult Literacy Level 1
- Adult Literacy Level 2
- Adult Numeracy Level 1
- Adult Numeracy Level 2.

These are all test-only qualifications with no portfolio, but the same tests are used for Adult Literacy and Adult Numeracy and for Key Skills Communication and Application of Number (see chart on pages 10–12). This means that students can:

- move on to a Key Skills qualification by completing a portfolio
- still gain a qualification if they start Key Skills but don't complete a portfolio.

There is a charge for transferring between qualifications, but students receive a certificate upon passing the test and portfolio.

There are **significant advantages** to teaching Adult Literacy and Adult Numeracy in schools. Students who would formerly have left school with few qualifications have the opportunity to achieve **accreditation and success** while schools experience an improvement in their threshold position in the Achievement and Accreditation Tables.

Adult Literacy and Adult Numeracy increases **student motivation** and provides a more favourable assessment method for those who find difficulty with traditional examinations. Young people can justifiably feel a real sense of achievement as they gain certification that meets employer needs.

Adult Literacy and Adult Numeracy qualifications can also **contribute to GCSE achievement**. Adult Literacy and Adult Numeracy Level 1 are each worth 12.5 points. Each Level 2 is worth 23 points. This compares with Short Course GCSE Grade E 14 points and Grade B 23 points.

Adult Literacy and Numeracy Tests	Key Skills qualification	GCSE	GNVQ	NVQ
Level 1	Level 1	D–G grade	Foundation	Level 1
Level 2	Level 2	A*–C grade	Intermediate	Level 2

Schools benefit from an improved position on the **Achievement and Attainment Tables** as each Adult Literacy and Adult Numeracy qualification contributes 10% towards threshold.

"We offer Adult Literacy and Numeracy to our Year 11 pupils and 64% achieved both at Level 2 making a 2% difference to our Level 2 threshold on the Achievement and Attainment Tables. These qualifications have made a significant improvement in our average point scores where Adult Literacy and Numeracy were in the best eight qualifications listed. We intend to enter every pupil for these tests next year and are very pleased that we are offering them at our school."

Jeff Sturrock, Assistant Head Teacher,
Biddick Sports College.

The test

The tests can be taken either on paper (12 opportunities per year) or on-screen (any day, any time), and the same items are used for both paper-based and on-screen tests. There are also Entry Level qualifications available as paper-based tests.

There are 40 questions and all are multiple choice. The Literacy test lasts 1 hour (Numeracy, 1 hour 15 minutes) and instant provisional results are provided at the end of the test. If the result is a pass, papered results (Individual Results Notice or IRN) and a certificate are issued within ten working days. There is no limit to the number of times a student can sit a test, although a fee is payable for every test taken.

Detailed results feedback is available through Edexcel Online (www.edexcelonline.co.uk). For more information, contact the Edexcel Online Customer Support Team on 0870 240 9819.

More support from Edexcel

The Skills for Life team provides regular e-mail updates and centre support packs. The Edexcel Information Manual provides information about administration arrangements. See www.edexcel.org.uk/sfc/emp-tp/infomanual/keyskills.

You can get further support for implementing the qualification from Edexcel.

- Website: www.edexcel.org.uk
- E-mail: skillsforlife@edexcel.org.uk
- Telephone: 0870 240 9800
- Regional Support: salessupport@edexcel.org.uk.

Other resources

There is a wide range of learning materials available from many websites. For example:

- Basic Skills Agency: www.basic-skills.co.uk
- Readwrite plus: www.dfes.gov.uk/readwriteplus
- Design your own practice tests: www.itembank.org.uk
- BBC Skillswise: www.bbc.co.uk/skillswise.

Coverage of national standards

The chart below indicates how the sections of the Skills Book map across to the national standards for reading and writing. For details of coverage of speaking and listening, see the charts at the beginning of each section in this book.

Standard	Skills Book Section	Skills Book page	Teacher's Handbook Section and page
Rt: Reading comprehension			
Rt1.1 Trace and understand main events of continuous descriptive, explanatory and persuasive texts	A2: Skimming a text to get an overview of what it is about A3: Reading a text carefully to get a detailed understanding of what the writer is saying A5: Identifying the main points of paragraphs	6 8 12	A: page 26
	B2: Understanding headings, subheadings and points to find information in continuous texts	20	B: page 34
	C3: Understanding descriptive texts C4: Understanding explanatory texts C5: Understanding persuasive texts	36 38 40	
Rt1.2 Recognise how language and other textual features are used to achieve different purposes, e.g. instruct, explain, describe, persuade	B1: Recognising the different features a text can have B2: Understanding how headings, subheadings, bullet points and paragraphs work B3: Understanding the features of a list B4: Understanding the features of charts and tables	18 20 22 24	
	C1: Recognising the different purposes that texts have C2: Recognising the features of instructive texts C3: Recognising the features of description texts C4: Recognising the features of explanation texts C5: Recognising the features of persuasive texts	32 34 36 38 40	C: page 42
Rt1.3 Identify main points and specific detail, and infer meaning from images which is not explicit in the text	A1: Scanning to find key words A2: Skimming to get an overview of the main points A3: Reading carefully to get a detailed understanding A5: Identifying the main point A6: Identifying a specific detail B2: Understanding headings, subheadings and bullet points B3: Finding information in a list B4: Finding information in charts or tables B5: Understanding what an image adds to a text	4 6 8 12 14 20 22 24 26	
Rt1.4 Use organisational and structural features to locate information	B2: Understanding how headings, subheadings, bullet points and paragraphs are used to structure texts B3: Understanding how information is organised in a list B4: Understanding how information is organised in charts and tables	20 22 24	B: page 34

Standard	Skills Book Section	Skills Book page	Teacher's Handbook Section and page
Rt1.5 Use different reading strategies to find and obtain information	A1: Scanning for key words A2: Skimming to find out what a text is about A3: Reading carefully for detailed understanding A5: Identifying the main point by skimming and close reading A6: Identifying a specific detail by skimming, scanning and reading carefully B1: Recognising different features in a text B2: Understanding how headings, subheadings and bullet points can be used to find information B3: Understanding how to find information in a list B4: Understanding how to find information in charts and tables	4 6 8 12 14 18 20 22 24	A: page 26
Rw: Vocabulary, word recognition and phonics			
Rw1.1 Use reference materials to find meanings of unfamiliar words	A4: Working out what a word means	10	A: page 26
Rw1.2 Recognise and understand the vocabulary associated with different types of text			C: page 42
Rw1.3 Recognise and understand an increasing range of vocabulary			D: page 50
Rs: Grammar and Punctuation			
Rs1.1 Use implicit and explicit grammatical knowledge			F: page 66
Ws: Grammar and Punctuation			
Ws1.1 Write in complete sentences			E: page 58
Ws1.2 Use correct grammar			F: page 66
Ws1.3 Punctuate sentences correctly and use punctuation so that meaning is clear			E: page 58
Wt: Writing composition			
Wt1.1 Plan and draft writing	B2: Understanding headings, subheadings and bullet points E4: Understanding when to begin a new paragraph	20 66	
Wt1.2 Judge how much to write and the level of detail to include	The skills covered in these books can be used to contribute to students' writing work		
Wt1.3 Present information in logical sequence; use paragraphs where appropriate	B2: Understanding headings, subheadings and bullet points E4: Understanding when to begin a new paragraph	20 66	B: page 34 C: page 42

Standard	Skills Book Section	Skills Book page	Teacher's Handbook Section and page
Wt1.4 Use language suitable for purpose and audience	C1: Recognising the purpose of a text C2: Recognising the features of instruction texts C3: Recognising the features of description texts C4: Recognising the features of explanation texts C5: Recognising the features of persuasive texts C6: Recognising the features of formal and informal texts C7: Understanding how to be formal	32 34 36 38 40 42 44	C: page 42
Wt1.5 Use format and structure for different purposes	B1: Recognising the different features in a text B2: Understanding how headings, subheadings and bullet points can be used to structure a text B3: Understanding how to organise information in a list B4: Understanding how to organise information in charts and tables	18 20 22 24	B: page 34
Wt1.6 Proof-read and revise writing for accuracy and meaning	D1: Spelling commonly used words correctly D2: Spelling words with common letter patterns correctly D3: Practising spotting spelling mistakes D4: Spotting words that sound the same but are spelt differently D5: Spelling what you mean E1: Understanding when to use a capital letter E2: Understanding how to end a sentence with the correct punctuation E3: Understanding how to write in complete sentences E4: Understanding when to begin a new paragraph F1: Understanding when to use different tenses F2: Making the subject and verb agree	48 50 52 54 56 60 62 64 66 70 72	F: page 66
Ws: Grammar and punctuation			
Ws1.1 Write in complete sentences	E1: Understanding when to use a capital letter E2: Understanding how to end a sentence with the correct punctuation E3: Understanding what makes up a complete sentence	60 62 64	
Ws1.2 Use correct grammar	F1: Understanding when to use different tenses F2: Making the subject and verb agree	70 72	
Ws1.3 Punctuate sentences correctly and use punctuation so that meaning is clear	E1: Understanding when to use a capital letter E2: Understanding how to end a sentence with the correct punctuation E3: Understanding how to write in complete sentences	60 62 64	

Standard	Skills Book Section	Skills Book page	Teacher's Handbook Section and page
Ww: Spelling and handwriting			
Ww1.1 Spell correctly words used in work, studies and daily life	D1: Spelling commonly used words correctly D2: Spelling words with common letter patterns correctly D3: Practising spotting spelling mistakes D4: Spotting words that sound the same but are spelt differently D5: Spelling what you mean	48 50 52 54 56	D: page 50
Ww1.2 Produce legible text	The skills covered in these books can be used to contribute to students' writing work		
SLlr: Listen and respond			
SLlr1.2 Listen for and understand explanations, instructions and narratives			C: page 42
SLlr1.4 Provide feedback and confirmation when listening to others			D: page 50 E: page 58
SLlr1.5 Make contributions relevant to the situation and the subject			F: page 66
SLc: Speak to communicate			
SLc1.1 Speak clearly in a way which suits the situation			B: page 34 C: page 42
SLc1.4 Present information and ideas			A: page 26 B: page 34
SLd: Engage in discussion			
SLd1.1 Follow and contribute to discussions			A: page 26

Mapping against Key Skills

The charts below maps Adult Literacy Level 1 standards against the National Curriculum and Key Skills Communication for Speaking and Listening, Reading and Writing.

Communication: Speaking and Listening

<table>
<tr><th rowspan="2">National Curriculum Level 5</th><th rowspan="2">Adult Literacy Level 1</th><th colspan="2">Key Skill – Level 1
C1.1</th></tr>
<tr><th>Part A</th><th>Part B</th></tr>
<tr><td rowspan="2">Pupils talk and listen confidently in a wide range of contexts, including some that are of a formal nature. Their talk engages the interest of the listener as they begin to vary their expression and vocabulary. In discussion, they pay close attention to what others say, ask questions to develop ideas and make contributions that take account of others' views. They begin to use Standard English in formal situations.</td><td rowspan="2">Listen and respond to spoken language, including information and narratives, and follow explanations and instructions of varying lengths, adapting response to speaker, medium and context.

Speak to communicate information, ideas and opinions, adapting speech and content to take account of the listeners(s) and medium.

Engage in discussion with one or more people in familiar and unfamiliar situations, making clear and relevant contributions that respond to what others say and produce a shared understanding about different topics.

In formal exchanges connected with education, training, work and social roles:
• listen for and identify relevant information from explanations and presentations on a range of topics
• listen for and understand explanations, instructions and narratives on different topics in a range of contexts
• use strategies to clarify and confirm understanding, e.g. facial expressions, body language and verbal prompts
• provide feedback and confirmation when listening to others
• make contributions relevant to the situation and the subject
• speak clearly in a way that suits the situation
• make requests and ask questions to obtain information in familiar and unfamiliar contexts
• respond to questions on a range of topics
• express clearly statements of fact, explanations, instructions, accounts and descriptions
• present information and ideas in a logical sequence and include detail and develop ideas where appropriate
• follow and contribute to discussions on a range of straightforward topics
• respect the turn-taking rights of others during discussions
• use appropriate phrases for interruption.</td><td>Discuss:
• Prepare for the discussion so that you can say things that are relevant.
• Judge when to speak and how much to say.
• Say things that suit the purpose of the discussion.
• Speak clearly in ways that suit the situation.
• Listen carefully and respond appropriately to what others say.</td><td>Take part in a either a one-to-one discussion or a group discussion:
1.1.1 Provide information that is relevant to the subject and purpose of the discussion.
1.1.2 Communicate clearly in a way that suits the situation and respond appropriately to others.</td></tr>
<tr><td colspan="2">Part C Guidance:
Discussion: To describe events, express opinions and develop ideas using language that everyone can understand, adapting your tone of voice, expression and manner to suit the formality of the situation.</td></tr>
</table>

Mapping against Key Skills – Communication: Reading

National Curriculum Level 5	Adult Literacy Level 1	Key Skill – Level 1 C2.2 Part A	Key Skill – Level 1 C2.2 Part B
Pupils show understanding of a range of texts, selecting essential points and using inference and deduction where appropriate. In their responses, they identify key features, themes and characters and select sentences, phrases and relevant information to support their views. They retrieve and collate information from a range of sources.	**Read and understand** straightforward texts of varying length on a variety of topics accurately and independently. **Read and obtain information** from different sources. In reports, instructional, explanatory and persuasive texts: • trace and understand the main events of continuous descriptive, explanatory and persuasive texts • recognise how language and other textual features are used to achieve different purposes, e.g. *to instruct, explain, describe, persuade* • identify the main points and specific detail, and infer meaning from images that is not explicit in the text • use organisational and structural features to locate information, e.g. *contents, index, menus, subheadings, paragraphs* • use different reading strategies to find and obtain information • use reference material to find the meaning of unfamiliar words.	**Read and obtain information:** • Identify the main points and ideas in different types of documents. • Obtain information from images. • Find out the meanings of words and phrases you do not understand. • Ask others when you are unclear about what you have read. **Part C Guidance:** **Read and obtain information:** To get instructions, facts, opinions and ideas from straightforward documents such as letters, memos, extracts from books, newspaper or magazine articles, and to collate this information as notes to use in discussions or in written material such as letters or short essays.	**Read and obtain information from at least one document.** 1.2.1 Read relevant material. 1.2.2 Identify accurately the main points and ideas. 1.2.3 Use the information to suit your purpose.

Mapping against Key Skills – Communication: Writing

<table>
<tr><th rowspan="2">National Curriculum Level 5</th><th rowspan="2">Adult Literacy Level 1</th><th colspan="2">Key Skill – Level 1
C1.3</th></tr>
<tr><th>Part A</th><th>Part B</th></tr>
<tr><td rowspan="2">Pupils' writing is varied and interesting, conveying meaning clearly in a range of forms for different readers, using a more formal style where appropriate. Vocabulary choices are imaginative and words are used precisely. Simple and complex sentences are organised into paragraphs. Words with complex regular patterns are usually spelt correctly. A range of punctuation, including commas, apostrophes and inverted commas, is usually used accurately. Handwriting is joined, clear and fluent and, where appropriate, is adapted to a range of tasks.</td><td rowspan="2">Write to communicate information, ideas and opinions clearly using length, format and style appropriate to purpose and audience.

In documents such as forms, records, e-mails, letters, narratives, instructions, reports, explanations:
• plan and draft writing
• judge how much to write and the level of detail to include
• present in a logical sequence, using paragraphs where appropriate
• use language suitable for purpose and audience
• use format and structure for different purposes
• write in complete sentences
• use correct grammar, e.g. subject-verb agreement, correct use of tense
• punctuate sentences correctly and use punctuation so that meaning is clear
• spell correctly words used most often in work, studies and daily life
• proof-read and revise writing for accuracy and meaning
• produce legible text.</td><td>Write documents:
• Use different formats for presenting information, including business letters, memos, forms and short reports.
• Judge the relevance of information and the amount of detail to include for your purpose.
• Use relevant images to help the reader understand your main points.
• Proof-read and where necessary redraft your documents so that:
– words you use most often in your work or studies and daily life are spelt correctly
– sentences are formed correctly with consistent use of tense and accurate subject-verb agreement such as 'she was' and 'we were'
– sentences are marked by capital letters, full stops and question marks
– your writing is organised into paragraphs where appropriate
– your meaning is clear.</td><td>Write two different types of documents.
1.3.1 Present relevant information in a format that suits your purpose.
1.3.2 Spell, punctuate and use grammar accurately.
1.3.3 Make your meaning clear.

Use at least one image, either to obtain information, or to convey information in your discussion or one of the documents you write to help the audience/reader understand the points you are making.</td></tr>
<tr><td colspan="2">Part C Guidance:
Write: To complete forms and produce documents such as business letters, memos, notes, short report or essays. To give or obtain facts, opinions and ideas.</td></tr>
</table>

Progression to Level 2

The chart below shows how the standards at Level 1 are developed at Level 2, expecting students to deal with a wider variety of and more complicated instructions, texts and situations.

Level 1	Level 2
Speaking and listening	
Listen and respond to spoken language, including information and narratives, and follow explanations and instructions of varying lengths, adapting response to speaker, medium and context	**Listen and respond** to spoken language, including **extended** information and narratives, and follow **detailed** explanations and **multi-step** instructions of varying length, adapting response to speaker, medium and context
Speak to communicate information, ideas and opinions, adapting speech and content to take account of the listener(s) and medium	**Speak to communicate** **straightforward and detailed** information, ideas and opinions **clearly**, adapting speech and content to take account of the listener(s), medium, **purpose and situation**
Engage in discussion with one or more people in familiar and unfamiliar situations, making clear and relevant contributions that respond to what others say and produce a shared understanding about different topics	**Engage in discussion** with one or more people **in a variety of different situations**, making clear and **effective contributions that produce outcomes appropriate to purpose and topic**
Reading	
Read and understand straightforward texts of varying length on a variety of topics accurately and independently	**Read and understand** **a range of texts** of varying **complexity** accurately and independently
Read and obtain information from different sources	**Read and obtain information** **of varying length and detail** from different sources
Writing	
Write to communicate information, ideas and opinions clearly using length, format and style appropriate to purpose and audience	**Write to communicate** information, ideas and opinions clearly and **effectively**, using length, format and style appropriate to purpose, **content** and audience

Answers to Skills Book activities

Section A Ways of reading

1 Scanning for key words

1 *open question*

2 vegetarian, onion, pepper, mushroom, sweetcorn, pineapple, chilli, tomato, olive

3 chicken, tuna, beef, pepperoni, ham

4 Cheese and tomato, Vegetarian, Veggie deluxe, Four cheeses

5 Meat Mountain, Italian Burnout, Feel The Heat

6

Topping	In how many pizzas?
Chicken	4
Mushroom	3
Red Onion	6
Sweetcorn	2
Pineapple	1

2 Skimming to find out what a text is about

1 C Being able to rent as many DVDs as you like for a month ☑

2 **C** Visit the Screen Select website to get your free DVD rental ☑

3 'Daisy is Missing' – **C** Mike wants to know if you have found his missing cat

'Corn on the cob' – **D** How to cook cobs of corn

'Be there!' – **F** How to enter a competition to win the chance to watch the FA Cup Final.

3 Reading carefully for detailed understanding

1 C People with strong views and who speak their mind – 'Do you want the opportunity to enforce your opinions on the rest of the nation?', 'Do you say what you like, and like what you say?'

D People who will get angry about things but don't mind being famous – 'Do you love nothing better than a good argument?', 'Do you want to be part of the most talked about TV show of 2006?'

2 **B** Big Brother is making a donation to charity, which will be divided between Shelter (who help people find and keep a home and campaign for decent housing for all), the Teenage Cancer Trust (who provide specialist units for teenagers) and a third charity to be chosen by the winner. ☑

4 Working out what a word means

1 C money back ☑

2 a) **C** making popcorn ☑

B collecting all the tools you need ☑

b) **A** kitchen equipment ☑

3 a) first plan

b) not pure

c) strong wish

5 Identifying the main point

1 B Gav wants to remove some graffiti and AJ tells him how. ☑

2 **C** A website says hairspray can be used to remove marker pen stains. ☑

3 **A** Graffiti can make small businesses leave an area. 4

B Graffiti can make an area feel depressing. 1

C Graffiti is expensive because it costs so much to remove it. 3

D Areas covered with graffiti are likely to become crime hot spots. 2

4 **B** Graffiti can make an area become poorer and more troubled. ☑

6 Identifying a specific detail

1 ✗ 29th May (Monday) Manchester (Egerton Youth Club, Knutsford)

2 29th May (Monday) Manchester (Egerton Youth Club, Knutsford)

3 The course is running in Manchester on 29th May

4 a) six seasons

b) Shay Given and Stephen Harper

c) Simon Smith Goalkeeping

d) 8–18

5 **B** Tackling and scoring

7 Test your skills

1 C ☑ to explain about mehndi for people who do not know what it is

2 C ☑ traditionally to celebrate special occasions

3 C ☑ the young leaves and twigs of a shrub

4 B ☑ Ireland

5 B ☑ long-established

Section B Understanding how texts are organised

1 Recognising different features in texts

1

Feature	Tells readers	E-mail	Letter	Memo	Instruction	Chart	Advert
Main heading	This is the main idea of the whole text.	B ✓	E	C ✓	D ✓	F ✓	A ✓
Subheading	This is the main point of this part of the text.						
Numbering	You need to understand the points in this order.				✓		
Bullet points	These are different points.			✓			
Paragraphs	The sentences in this part are all about the same idea.	✓	✓				✓

2 Understanding headings, subheadings and points

1 1 <u>The office party</u> – **Numbering**

2 <u>Seasonal cards</u> – **Numbering**

3 <u>Festive gifts</u> – **Numbering**

a Date: Friday 20 December or Saturday 21 December. – **Letters**

b Zara to find suitable venue offering – **Letters**

c Taylor to check whether people want to bring partners. – **Letters**

a No cards. Jack to make people aware of alternative: putting a message on the board and giving money to charity instead. – **Letters**

b Organise central message board. – **Letters**

c Collect donations. – **Letters**

a Rosh to distribute presents on 21 December. – **Letters**

- good meal – reasonably priced – **Bullet points**
- band or disco – **Bullet points**
- somewhere easy to get home from by bus – **Bullet points**
- Senior Management will get blue and gold packages. – **Bullet points**
- Supervisors will get red and green packages. – **Bullet points**
- All other staff will get yellow and orange packages. – **Bullet points**

Meeting notes from 3 October 2007 – Main heading
<u>The office party</u> – **Subheading**
<u>Seasonal cards</u> – **Subheading**
<u>Festive gifts</u> – **Subheading**

2 3 <u>Festive gifts</u>

a Rosh to distribute presents on December 21.

- *Senior Management* will get blue and gold packages.
- *Supervisors* will get red and green packages.
- *All other staff* will get yellow and orange packages.

3 subheading – Timetable

heading – KARTING MORNING

bullet point –
- wear old clothes
- bring £1 for the locker and money for lunch if you are staying
- be prepared to have fun!

first paragraph – We hope you are looking forward to our team-building day on Saturday. A map and travel details are attached to this letter.

second paragraph – Everyone needs to arrive on time so we can get the most out of the morning. There is a café on site so if you can stay on for lunch we could all eat there.

points in time order –

9.00–9.15 a.m. Arrive and get dressed in helmets and padding
9.15–10.00 What is Kart racing?
10.00–10.20 How a Kart works
10.30–11.30 Practice runs
11.30–12.30 Races

points in random order –

- wear old clothes
- bring £1 for the locker and money for lunch if you are staying
- be prepared to have fun!

3 Searching through a list

1 A They are in random/alphabetical/numerical order.

B First the list has in bold print the band's name/ place where the band is playing/telephone number.

Then the list has the band's name/place where the band is playing/telephone number.

Last you are told the band's name/place where the band is playing/telephone number.

2 a) Hope of the States

b) Rescue the Astronauts, The Winding Stair, Amoruza

c) 01224 624642

d) Junction

3 a) 1 support or help

b) backpack

c) 2 a musical accompaniment, especially for a singer

d) background

4 a) 3

b) 10.00 5.00 10.00

c) 8.00

d) horse racing from USA, Australian Rugby League

4 Finding information in charts or tables

1 b) Comic Relief

c) February

d) Evie Parts 1, 2 and 3

e) McFly Tony Christie featuring Peter Kay

2 **B** The air ambulance attends more medical emergencies than cardiac arrests. ☑

D The air ambulance helps more people injured while horse riding than people injured at work or on a farm. ☑

E The air ambulance is mostly called out to road traffic accidents. ☑

3 b) 13.20
c) 13.43 ✗
d) 12.43 ✓
e) 12.13

4 a) 6p
b) 12p
c) 12p
d) 15p per minute
e) 10p per minute

5 **A** Calls made to your favourite number on Standard tariff are more expensive than on Enjoy! Super tariff. ☒

B Texts made on Extra tariff are cheaper than on Enjoy! Super tariff. ☒

C Texts costs most on the Standard tariff. ☑

5 Understanding what an image adds to a text

1 **D** They show how easy it is to recycle an ink cartridge. ☑

2 a) An adventurous 8-year-old. [3]

b) A girl who secretly wishes she could be a celebrity. [2]

c) An adult who quite enjoys feeling scared but hates bad language. [4]

d) A man who hates violence. [1]

6 Test your skills

1 **D** ☑ To help readers find different pieces of information.

2 **C** ☑ What the pudding is like and how to vary it.

3 **B** ☑ It shows readers how to toss the pancakes.

4 **C** ☑ the order in which they need to be carried out.

C Understanding what writers want their readers to do

1 Recognising the purpose of a text

1 **B** – information

D – instruction

C – description

E – explanation

A – persuasive

2 Recognising the features of instruction texts

1 This text tells readers how to make *flapjacks*

Most of the sentences are commands (stir, bake) that begin with a *verb*.

These words are used to *link and sequence* ideas.

These *numbers* tell you information in the order you need to follow it.

2 **A** – Protect your pet when fireworks are around by following our animal friendly firework code.

B – Protect / Keep / Close / Leave / Make sure

C – Close all windows and curtains. Then switch on music or television to drown out the noise.

D – • Keep / • Close / • Leave / • Make sure

3 a) **A** at the beginning ☑

b) **C** numbered points ☑

c) **B** The points do not have to be followed in any particular order. ☑

3 Understanding description texts

1 **B** – *For example* Aged 23 / height 195 cm / medium build / wearing dark blue jeans, new white trainers and a black sports top with a hood

C – dark blue / new white / black

2 sight, hearing

3 (beautiful) (white) (blue)

4 They sound worse than your brother's band!

5 **C** a mixed experience ☑

6 a) thick, overpowering

b) (terrified)

7 **B** frightening ☑

4 Understanding explanation texts

1 **2** – Therefore, Since

3 – To stand a chance of being picked all you have to do is sign up with a good agency of extras, who will ask you to give them a CV and photograph; casting agencies are not looking for exam results because what they want are people who will make their scene look right, who can get up early, are totally reliable and will get on and do the job

2 because ✓
so which means ✓
this means that ✓

3 a) 2

b) 1

c) **A** benefit staff ☑

5 Understanding persuasive texts

1 a) B To give money to the charity that looks after dogs. ☑

b) *Two of:* Your gift will help, your pound means that, we'll send you photos and news, You'd receive so much love in return, you'll have a friend for life

c) Yes ☑
You'd receive so much love in return ★
You'll have a friend for life ★

d) (pity) (love) (sadness) (kindness)

e) (colour) (capitals)

2 a) visit Blue Horizons Shopping and Leisure

b) *For example:* if you're looking for that, If you've overindulged, if you just want to chill out, If you just fancy

c) *Four of:* the ultimate provides a great atmosphere, Blue Horizons has it all, tickle your taste buds, We have a fantastic gym with up to the minute equipment

d) (greed) (love) (enjoyment)

e) (colour) (CAPITALS) (italics)

6 Formal and informal texts

1 gives the info

2 wanna, fags

3 *Suggested answer:* mate: friend
she'd: she had
Suggested answer: chucking it down: raining heavily
&: and
Suggested answer: was/goin': /was travelling at
couldn't: could not control the car
Suggested answer: went kinda skiddin: started to skid
b4: before

4

it/has	*there is*	*are not*
(it's)	(there's)	(aren't)
will not	*through*	
(won't)	(thro')	

5 *at lunch*
for the purpose of taking my midday meal

I'd love
I would very much like

your invite
your kind invitation

see
view

watch a film and eat takeaway pizza
in order to view a film and eat pizza delivered to your door:

Love
Yours sincerely

7 Choosing to be formal

1 a) I b) F c) I d) F

2 **A** Jade
B Yours sincerely
C Jade Stone
Yours sincerely / Yours truly / Best wishes / Kind regards

3 a) F b) I c) I d) F

4 a) **A** I ☑ **B** F ☑ **C** F ☑
b) **B** I'm sure it'll be a fab day.
C They have gone bust.

8 Test your skills

1 **C** ☑ to persuade
2 **A** ☑ To make those words stand out
3 **C** ☑ cash
4 **D** ☑ lines 19–21

D Spelling words correctly

1 Learning to spell commonly used words

1 1 because 2 which 3 until
4 knew 5 friend 6 sight
7 separate

2 Open question.

3 1 necessary 2 Wednesday 3 February
4 receive 5 unusual 6 sincerely
7 different

2 Spelling words with common letter patterns correctly

1 a) relief, thief, Chief, grief
receive, receipt, eight
plough, through, rough, cough
cancelling, marvellous, travelling
Quickly, quietly, quivering, Queen
gnat, gnawing, sign
knew, knight, kneeling
sighed, bright, light, slightly, high

b) achieve, believe, relieve
veil, weird, weight, ceiling, height
although, dough, enough, rough, roughly
called, calling, filled, filling, telling, rebelled, rebelling, rebellious
quite, quiet, quick, quiz, question
design, resign, align, gnome, gnarled
knob, knit, knife, knot, knock, know
might, mighty, ought, nought, though, naughty, sigh, sight, sighting

Tough cop Rock Adam receives a mysterious mobile phone call just before he begins his late shift. The caller warns him to stay in tonight if he wants to avoid being caught and injured in a major gang fight. Rock believes the caller is his wife – but she's been dead for five years, or has she?

Tracing the mobile phone call to a billiard hall in a rough neighbourhood, Rock knocks on doors to ask lots of questions. He starts his enquiries and soon discovers everyone is afraid of the quiet barman at the billiard hall. Even the Chief of Police seems to be deceiving Rock as the plot twists and turns, keeping you guessing right up to the end.

3 Practising spotting spelling mistakes

1 a) My friend is a CCTV operator in a (goverment) building. government
b) The CCTV cameras had (tapped) a crime taking place. taped
c) A hooded thief took a large (amout) of computer hardware. amount
d) On three (ocasions) the hooded thief was filmed at the back door. occasions
e) In a (seprate) shot, the thief was caught with his hood down. separate
f) It was not (neccesary) to start a search. necessary
g) The thief was (defanately) a man who lived down the street. definitely

missing letters	a), c), d), e), f)
incorrect letter	g)
single letters where there should be double letters	d), f)
double letters where there should be a single letter	f)

2 **A** unusul ☑
3 **A** address ☑
4 (intrested)
5 surfise
6 **B** achieve ☑
7 (thoroghly)
8 **D** **wearing** ☑

4 Spotting words that sound the same but are spelt differently

1 *Open question*

2 a) I want to have a barbecue this evening.
b) We will need to cook at least two packets of burgers for everyone.
c) If you go to Savalot they are selling two for the price of one so you will save two pounds.
d) We could get two packages of sausages to cook, too.
e) I just want to check if my team-mates can come too.
f) Do you think starting at 8.00 p.m. is too late?

3 Lee went (two) *to* Savalot (too) *to* buy the sausages. They were offering two for the price of one. He couldn't decide if (to) *two* packets would be (two) *too* much. He phoned his friend to check. She said he needed (too) *to* buy four packets not two.

4 a) When we got there all the food was cooked already.
b) I was so pleased to see there was a chocolate fudge brownie pudding too.
c) Their friends are really nice people.
d) They're going to ask me to do some babysitting for them.
e) Lee said their garden was too small for all their friends to fit in.

5 I like going to their house because most of (they're) friends are really chatty. I feel a bit shy with people if (their) a bit quiet too. Lee's friends are really into dancing. They're always jumping up when he puts (there) favourite music on. (Their) are a couple of really nice girls who always get my mum and auntie up on (they're) feet too.

6 I could have stayed longer but (there)/their/they're was the morning to think about. I had to be up early and get down (to)/too/two the shop by seven or I would be to/(too)/two late (to)/too/two start work. Lee said the last people left at to/too/(two) o'clock but (there)/their/they're was a lot of clearing up to do. He thought it was great, except for having to clear up.

5 Spelling what you mean

1 a) Turn of/(off) the tap when you brush your teeth!
b) In one day you will('ve)/of saved a lot of water.
c) Shop with us! We (accept)/except all major credit cards.
d) You can use all major credit cards accept/(except) for American Express.

2

1	knew	new
2	Knight	night
3	where	wear
4	Flour	Flower
5	your	you're
6	I	eye
7	bald	bold
8	must of	must have
9	there	their
10	currant	current
11	except	accept
12	Right	Write
13	two	to

6 Test your skills

1	B ✓	line 10
2	C ✓	furniture
3	B ✓	too
4	A ✓	there
5	B ✓	single in line 15
6	A ✓	through

E Punctuation

1 Capital letters

1 *Open question*

2 Really Cool Yule – Begin the title of a show or event with a capital letter.

I promise – the pronoun I should always be a capital letter.

Trim Z Fringe – Begin the name of a particular person place or organisation with a capital letter.

TJ – Initials should always be in capital letters.

Wanda Frill – Begin the name of a particular person place or organisation with a capital letter.

Christmas – Begin the days of the week, months and special occasions with a capital letter.

November – Begin the days of the week, months and special occasions with a capital letter.

3 Toby Childs, We, *Allstars Magazine*, Say, Fann, She, Tuesday's

4 *Open question*

2 Ending sentences

1 *Open question*

2 a) Which English captain stood down after the 2006 World Cup?
   b) Can I phone a friend?
   c) I think it was Wayne Rooney.
   d) Is that your final answer?
   e) What do you think you will do with your £100 prize?

3 Are you a decorator who is hard working and experienced? Do you want your home left clean and tidy? Look no further! Call Mark Walls on 324774. References are available.

4 **C** lines 5 and 8 ☑

3 Making sense of sentences

1 a) Welcome to the Computer Warehouse. ☑
   b) Our July Buyer's Guide. ☒
   c) As you'd expect, we have the widest range of computers in the UK. ☑
   d) Your shopping easy. ☒
   e) We have some fantastic new savings this summer. ☑

2 Castlehill is a well-organised site and it has wonderful views over the cove. The site has three shops and a restaurant, and boasts a heated outdoor swimming pool. The coast is easily accessible, but elderly visitors may find the steps to the cove challenging.

3 a) The night life is good. There are lots of discos. ☑
   b) There is a shop on site, but it is probably expensive. ☑
   c) We could rent a caravan. It is probably cheaper. ☑

4 **D** for anything, but no one could ☑

5 **B** then

4 Starting a new paragraph

1 b) 9
   c) the last party
   d) it is about a different event

2 arrangements. // Afterwards

3 **B** There should be a new paragraph on line 5, because it mentions a different party ☑

5 Test your skills

1 **C** ☑ It is part of the title of an organisation.

2 **D** ☑ line 16

3 **C** ☑ lines 10–11

4 **D** ☑ line 20

5 **C** ☑ line 16

F Using good grammar

1 Using the right tense

1 a) (past)
   b) (present)
   c) (future)
   d) (past)

2 a) Yesterday he visited his sister.
   b) At the moment I am too busy.
   c) Nasim will do it next week.
   d) For the last three years we have visited Drayford Theme Park.

3 **B** were staying ☑

4 **C** was ☑

5 **A** started ☑

2 Making your subject and verb agree

1 a) They were eating ice cream. ☑
   b) Listen to what I am saying to you. ☑
   c) We were picked up by Dad at 9.30. ☑
   d) The house, which had two doors, was built of brick. ☑

2 c) 1 d) 1 e) 1 f) 3 g) 1

3 b) Unfortunately Danny Breaker (sound) more like the footballer Maradona. ☒
   c) Adam and Jono (was) winners. ☒
   d) In round two they (have) to dance and sing in a West End musical. ☑

4 When Adam Stone, in a sparkling gold suit, walks on stage the fans (cheers). But as he (sing) 'Memories' they start laughing. He cannot reach the high notes. Jonno Becks is better, but when he (dance) he slips over and knocks down part of the scenery. At the end of round two they (has) drawn.

5 **C** third ☑

3 Test your skills

1 **C** ☑ line 3

2 **D** ☑ line 7

3 **B** ☑ line 2

4 **D** ☑ went

Whole class progress tracking grid

Use the chart below to track when each of your students has complete a section in the Skills Book and what their score is in the end of section test.

	A Reading for information and understanding		**B Understanding the features of different texts**		**C Understanding how writers achieve their purpose**		**D Spelling words correctly**		**E Punctuation**		**F Grammar**		**G Preparing for the test**	
Student Name	Completed	Score	Completed	Score	Completed	Score	Completed	Score	Completed	Score	Completed	Score	Completed	Score

Whole class progress tracking grid

	A Reading for information and understanding		B Understanding the features of different texts		C Understanding how writers achieve their purpose		D Spelling words correctly		E Punctuation		F Grammar		G Preparing for the test	
Student Name	Completed	Score	Completed	Score	Completed	Score	Completed	Score	Completed	Score	Completed	Score	Completed	Score

Certificate

Awarded to

For successfully completing a course in

Adult Literacy Level 1

Date: ....

Signed: ....

A Ways of reading

(pages 4–17 in the Skills Book)

Speaking and Listening	Reading	Writing
SLd/L1.1 Follow and contribute to discussions on a range of straightforward topics. ***SLc/L1.4*** Present information and ideas in a logical sequence and include detail and develop ideas.	***Rt/1.3*** Identify main points and specific detail; infer meaning from images which is not explicit in the text. ***Rt/1.5*** Use different reading strategies to find and obtain information. ***Rw/1.1*** Use reference materials to find meanings of unfamiliar words.	***Wt/L1.6*** Proof-read and revise. ***Wt/1.5*** Use format and structure for different purposes.

Coverage of standards

The chart above lists the coverage of standards in Section A of the Level 1 Skills Book. It also lists additional standards that could be taught with this section, using the suggestions below.

Section outline

Section A covers a range of reading skills that will be assessed in the ALAN test. Poor readers will need a great deal of support in order to learn these skills. Good readers will already use many of these skills intuitively but will find that their test performances improves once they understand the skills more explicitly.

The reading skills covered are:

- skimming, scanning and close reading
- understanding difficult words
- finding main points and details.

Approaches to teaching

You will need to teach two important concepts in this section:

- there are different reading skills, which are used for different purposes
- if students actively engage with texts, rather than read passively, they will understand a great deal more.

Encourage students to decide which reading skill they need to use to answer a particular question in the test. This will save them time. For example, a question may be answered by skimming or scanning the text and close reading may not be necessary.

Whole class tip

Approach some of the tests in this book as whole class activities and encourage the pupils to identify the reading skill or skills that each question is testing.

It is important to teach the students how to read a text actively. Encourage students to become used to reading texts with a pen, and annotating the text while they are reading. This will help them **engage** with the text, rather than just passively read it.

As the students become more confident readers they should be able to annotate:

- **words or phrases** that might answer the test questions
- **words** they do not know, which may need thought when answering questions
- **topic sentences** that define the subject of a paragraph and help to identify the main points of a text
- **connectives**, i.e. words or phrases that link ideas together, such as *however, secondly, in addition*. Identifying connectives helps students to see the relationship between ideas in a text.

When preparing students for the test, teach them to read the questions before they start to read the text. This will mean their reading has a purpose – to answer specific questions. It is easier to read a text if you know why you are reading it.

The most important thing you can do is to model reading skills with students. You can do this with individuals or with the whole class, using an OHP or digital projector.

- Choose one of the tests and talk about your thought processes as you read it.
- Explain how you skim and scan, and how the two skills are different.
- Explain how you make sense of difficult words.

Above all, show that you sometimes have problems answering questions but that you can engage with the text in order to work things out.

Linked Speaking and Listening and Writing activities

This section will give you the opportunity to target relevant Speaking and Listening and Writing standards, using activities such as the ones explored below.

Speaking and Listening

- Give students a short piece of text about an issue, such as that about graffiti on page 13 of the Level 1 Skills Book. Ask students to create a list of reasons why people might want a wall of artistic graffiti and a list of reasons why they might object to it. Students may feed back their ideas following discussion *(SLd/L1.1)*.
- Give students a sequence of paragraphs from an information text, such as that on page 15 of the Level 1 Skills Book. These should be cut out and presented out of order for students to rearrange into the correct order. Students should put the paragraphs in order and explain why they have made their choices *(SLc/L1.4)*.

Writing

- Ask students to identify five words in a passage of their own writing, then to change the five words, either adding to them or improving them using a thesaurus. They should indicate changes or improvements by highlighting the original word and writing the amendment or addition in the margin *(Wt/L1.6)*.
- Give students a piece of text without headings, subheadings or a specific layout. Ask them to design a layout and add organisational features that will help readers work their way around the text. The article about graffiti on page 13 of the Level 1 Skills Book could be used for this *(Wt/L1.5)*.

Photocopiable worksheets

The following photocopiable sheets are included for Section A:

A1 Skimming, scanning and close reading

A2 Scanning for meaning

A3 Working out what a word means

A4 Identifying the main points

A5 Identifying a specific detail

A6 Finding a specific detail.

A1 Skimming, scanning and close reading

This worksheet accompanies **p.4–9** in the *Level 1 Skills Book*

Name ____________________ Date __________

1 Look at the following definitions. Draw a line to each definition to the reading skill it describes.

Skimming is...	reading in detail, focusing in on most of what you read.
Scanning is...	reading over a whole text at speed, not reading every word but searching for key words.
Close reading is...	reading quickly through a text to get an overview of what it is about.

2 Look at the skills listed below. Add a code to show whether you would use it when you are skimming (sk), scanning (sc) or reading closely (r-c).

________ Highlight words or sentences

________ Look at illustrations and pictures

________ Look at longer words that stand out

________ Look at the headings and subheadings

________ Look at topic sentences in each paragraph

________ Look for bold text or italics

________ Look for key words

________ Look for numbers

________ Look for diagrams or charts

________ Read more slowly

________ Read the introduction more carefully

________ Underline important words

Literacy Teacher's Handbook Level 1 © Edexcel Limited 2006

A2 Scanning for meaning

This worksheet accompanies **p.4–5** in the *Level 1 Skills Book*

Name ______________________ Date ____________

You are going to create a scanning test for another student. Using the menu below, create five questions that a difficult customer in the restaurant might ask. For example, you might ask, "Which pizzas don't have mushrooms?" or "Do you have any vegetarian pasta dishes?"

1 ______________________

2 ______________________

3 ______________________

4 ______________________

5 ______________________

Now test your questions on another student. They have to scan the menu to answer your questions.

Starters

Antipasto Misto A selection of salami, meats, salad, ripe vine tomatoes and mozzarella.

Caesar Salad A mix of fresh salad leaves, strips of chicken and smoked bacon, with an olive oil dressing.

Funghi al aglio Button mushrooms, lightly sautéed then covered with a garlic and parsley dressing.

Pasta dishes

Lasagne Layers of meat and tomato sauce, sandwiched between sheets of pasta and bechamel sauce.

Pasta Primavera Pasta topped with fresh vegetables, including peas, beans, carrots and broccoli.

Pasta Milanese Pasta shells topped with a rich, spicy meat sauce, fresh herbs and grated parmesan cheese.

Pizzas

Pizza Margherita A thin-crust pizza with a rich tomato and herb base, covered with mozzarella.

Pizza Casa Mia A speciality pizza with fresh tomatoes, mozzarella, salami, ham, roasted peppers, onions and sweetcorn.

Pizza Napoli A deep-pan pizza with tomatoes, mushrooms and olives, and topped with mozzarella.

Desserts

Ice cream Our house speciality is Neapolitan: a blend of chocolate, strawberry and vanilla, but we also serve pistachio, toffee or cherry in a combination of your choice.

Tiramisu Layers of chocolate, coffee and cream sandwiched between soft sponge cake.

Fruit Salad Our fruit salad includes bananas, apples, grapes, cherries, strawberries and kiwi fruit.

A3 Working out what a word means

This worksheet accompanies **p.10–11** in the *Level 1 Skills Book*

Name ______________________ Date __________

1 Read the hotel description below and work out what the words in bold mean.

2 For each bold word in the description, choose a word from the box below that means the same and write it alongside the line in which you would want to use it.

large	lovely	equipment	big	has	many	use

The Hotel Beau Rivage is situated near the **delightful** town of Illetas in Majorca. Illetas is a pleasant little town, 5 miles from the main city of Palma. You will find shops, tavernas and **numerous** restaurants in Illetas itself, although if you are looking for a wider range of shops and activities, you may wish to travel into Palma. There are frequent buses from the hotel to Illetas which run every 30 minutes, or you may wish to hire a taxi from the hotel reception.

In the hotel grounds, there are two tennis courts, a mini-golf course, three swimming pools (including one for children), **extensive** gardens and several paved verandahs complete with sun loungers, umbrellas and waiter service. If the sun and sand is a little too much for you, the hotel **is equipped with** a range of spa facilities which you are free to use. These include an indoor pool, a spa bath and a hair and beauty salon. We can also offer appointments with a fully qualified physiotherapist. Guests can **take advantage of** the three restaurants, two bars and the ice-cream parlour as part of the price.

The rooms are **spacious** and all have a balcony with a view of the sea or gardens. Most rooms are doubles or twin rooms, and include tea and coffee-making **facilities**, satellite television, air-conditioning, a modern bathroom and access to the Internet. You can also make use of the mini-bar as you enjoy the views, should you wish.

Literacy Teacher's Handbook Level 1 © Edexcel Limited 2006

Identifying the main points

This worksheet accompanies **p.12–13** in the *Level 1 Skills Book*

Name ______________________________ Date ____________

1 Skim read this article about skateboarding. Underline words that you think sum up the main point of each paragraph.

2 Decide which word from the multiple-choice options to the right is most suitable to sum up each paragraph.

I'm really interested in skateboarding. I go skateboarding most evenings and I take my board out all day on Saturday. The thing I like most about skateboarding is the buzz of excitement you get if you do a really good trick, but I've also met a lot of my friends because of skateboarding, which has also been one of the reasons I keep on doing it. Your friends help you gain the confidence to do tricks and stunts on your skateboard, and they can also help show you how to do it.

Skateboarding has always been really popular. I think it really started in America in the 1950s around about the same time surfing became popular. The history of the skateboard probably came about when someone tried to make a surfboard you could use on land. This might be the reason it was first called 'sidewalk surfing'. It got really popular in the 1970s when it started to become a bit of a cult. Skater fashions developed, and even today you can often tell a skater by what they are wearing. Lots of skaters wear baggies or hooded tops with band names on.

In the past, skaters used to use whatever they could skate on to do their tricks, so many of the tricks used to be ones you could do without any specially-made structures or courses. Lots of skaters did jumps, grinds and slides. Now, skaters often use ramps and half-pipes and do things like no-hands aerial jumps where they come off the ramp. You have to be really good to do a jump like this! You need to go to a skate park to use ramps, unless your mum lets you build one in the back garden!

Paragraph 1

A ☐ Interests
B ☐ Tricks
C ☐ Excitement and friends
D ☐ Skateboarding

Paragraph 2

A ☐ Popularity
B ☐ History
C ☐ Skateboarding
D ☐ Fashions

Paragraph 3

A ☐ Tricks
B ☐ History
C ☐ Structures
D ☐ Ramps

A5 Identify a specific detail

This worksheet accompanies **p.14–15** in the *Level 1 Skills Book*

Name ______________________ Date __________

Some features, such as numbers, capital letters or words in bold, help us find specific details in a text.

1. Read carefully the advertisement at the bottom of the page for a goalkeeping course. In the first column of the table below, write a list of five questions that a reader may have about the course, such as "Who is Simon Smith?" Underline the answer in the text underneath.
2. Then in the second column write suggestions about how the writer could help the reader find specific details more quickly. One example has been done for you.

Questions a reader may ask	How to make the answer stand out
What skills are covered in the course?	*Use a bullet point and a new line for each skill.*

Simon Smith is one of the country's leading goalkeeping coaches. Simon spent six seasons as Sir Bobby Robson's goalkeeping coach at Newcastle United FC, working with the Republic of Ireland's Shay Given and Stephen Harper before moving abroad to work as a consultant to the Canadian Soccer Association.

The course will cover the main techniques and skills of goalkeeping: goalkeeping-specific warm ups, handling, footwork, diving, shot stopping, one v. one crossing, dealing with the back pass, distribution. These topics will be covered in realistic match-related practices, giving you the edge when you return to your team.

Course dates:

27th May (Saturday) Coventry (Alan Higgs Sports Centre)

28th May (Sunday) London (Metropolitan Police Club, Chigwell)

29th May (Monday) Manchester (Egerton Youth Club, Knutsford)

30th May (Tuesday) Newcastle (venue to be confirmed)

To find out more about these and other courses run by Simon Smith Goalkeeping, or to request an application form, call 0191 2526950 or log on to www.simonsmithgoalkeeping.com

Literacy Teacher's Handbook Level 1 © Edexcel Limited 2006

A6 Finding a specific detail

This worksheet accompanies **p.12–15** in the *Level 1 Skills Book*

Name ______________________ Date ____________

Features such as numbers, bold text, underlined text, words with capitals and words in italics stand out in a text and help the reader find specific details.

The writer of the advertisement at the bottom of the page has not used the features well and it is hard to read.

1 Look at the advertisement and find one example in the text of each of the features in the list below. Check whether they help to make the most important words stand out.

Check:

- use of numbers
- use of words all in capitals
- use of words beginning with capitals
- use of underlining
- use of italics
- use of bold
- use of highlighting.

2 Now choose the right place in the text for each feature from the list, circling where it should go and writing it alongside the appropriate place in the text.

Are you INTERESTED in skateboarding? If you are, Why Not Come to greenfields playing fields? There is a specially constructed half-pipe and slalom ramp where you can *practise* your skills.

It's two pounds fifty **to use the ramp**, and once you are in, you can use the ramps for 2 hours.

If you need more information, call zero two seven triple two treble seven or check out our website.

B Understanding how texts are organised

(pages 18–31 in the Skills Book)

Speaking and Listening	Reading	Writing
SLc/L1.4 Present information and ideas in a logical sequence and include detail and develop ideas. ***SLc/L1.1*** Speak clearly in a way which suits the situation.	***Rt/L1.1*** Trace and understand the main events of continuous descriptive, explanatory and persuasive texts. ***Rt/L1.4*** Use organisational and structural features to locate information, e.g. contents, index, menus, subheadings, paragraphs.	***Wt/L1.3*** Present information in a logical sequence, using paragraphs where appropriate. ***Wt/L1.5*** Use format and structure for different purposes.

Coverage of standards

The chart above lists coverage of standards in Section B of the Level 1 Skills Book. It also lists additional standards that could be taught with this section, using the suggestions below.

Section outline

Section B covers how writers use the structure and organisation of a text to help the reader. Students should understand how organisational features within a text can help a reader recognise how the ideas are built up.

The following skills are covered:

- understanding headings, subheadings and points
- organising a text
- finding information in charts and tables
- making sense of images.

Approaches to teaching

Two important concepts need to be taught in this section:

- how writers organise their texts to help the reader
- how information can be presented in other ways, such as tables, diagrams or images.

For example, you may wish to explore:

- how points are prioritised using bullets or numbering
- how headings and subheadings can be used to organise the writing.

Students should also explore how writers use paragraphs to shift the focus of ideas in the text, showing understanding of the way the writer breaks up the text.

When reading, students need to understand how to use organisational features of the text to help them identify what it is they will need to read. Students should become more adept at managing information that is presented in tables or charts, showing that they are able to find information quickly. They should begin to explore how images can add to a text, and how the image can support the meaning of the text.

When studying this unit, students will find it helpful if you can explain and discuss the purpose of the headings and subheadings, or the way the information has been presented.

Whole class tip

It is always helpful when the teacher models the process of exploring a text through shared or modelled reading. Students should then gain confidence through looking at a range of exemplar material in order to identify and comment on the way presentational features have been used. With this skill, pupils should become more adept at considering why the writer has organised a text in a particular way.

Linked Speaking and Listening and Writing activities

This unit will give you the opportunity to target relevant Writing and Speaking and Listening standards through activities such as the ones explored below.

Speaking and Listening

- Give students five topic sentences taken from a piece of informative writing, possibly taken from five different paragraphs or sections. These should be cut up so they can be rearranged. Students should decide on the order, explaining their reasons. Following this, they may discuss what information they think would be contained in the rest of the paragraph, giving reasons for their thoughts *(SLc/L1.4)*.
- Ask students to bring in an example of an informative, explanatory, instructive or persuasive text. They should pick out three reasons that helped them guess the text type and then present it to a listener, explaining the reasons for their thinking *(SLc/L1.1)*.

Writing

- Give students three paragraphs of text that have had the paragraph line breaks removed. Ask students to identify where the line breaks could go and how they know. These can be annotated on the text *(Wt/L1.3)*.
- Give students a copy of the objectives of a computer game. Ask students to use the same text, with up to five changes, to present the game to an adult market and a teenage market, using aspects of format and structure to help them design the text appropriately *(Wt/L1.5)*.

Photcopiable worksheets

The following photocopiable worksheets are included for Section B:

B1 Understand headings, subheadings and points 1

B2 Understand headings, subheadings and points 2

B3 Organise a text 1

B4 Organise a text 2

B5 Make sense of an image

B6 Understand headings, subheadings and points 3.

B1 Understand headings, subheadings and points 1

This worksheet accompanies **p.18–21** in the *Level 1 Skills Book*

Name ____________________ Date ________

1 Read the article at the bottom of the page. It summarises some of the main kinds of computer games that are available. The writer has not used any subheadings.

2 Scan the text and pick out a word or phrase in each paragraph that would help the reader identify what the paragraph is about. Add the word or phrase to the table below, then think of a subheading that the writer could use to help the reader. The first one has been done for you.

	Word or phrase to identify what the paragraph is about	Subheading
Paragraph 1	*Many kinds of computer games available nowadays*	*Today's computer games – a huge range*
Paragraph 2		
Paragraph 3		
Paragraph 4		

There are many kinds of computer games available nowadays. Times have moved on since the arcade games of the 1970s and 1980s. Today's computer game player has a huge range of games from which to choose. Since video games became popular in the 1970s, manufacturers have created games to suit everybody's need.

One of the most popular computer game types, or 'genres', is the role-playing game. In this type of game, you play as if you are a particular character. The character you choose to play will have a range of skills depending on what type of person they are. For instance, they might be better at weapons mastery or at stealth. In these games, the objective is to complete an adventure or quest.

Another type of game that's popular is a sports-based game. These cover any type of sport that you might imagine, such as football and rugby. If there's a particular sport you enjoy, you can guarantee there's a game based on it. You can either play a game where you are the manager of a team, which is a strategy-based game, or you can play a game where you are one of the players, known as 'electronic sports' because you are playing as if you are taking part in the sport.

Simulation games are also very popular. These are games that allow you to see how situations would develop over time. In games like this, you start off some kind of situation or create a business and develop it through history. You can build families, cities, businesses, hospitals, theme parks or even whole nations. Some simulation games are known as 'strategy games' where you play out situations like battles. Simulation games also cover games where you can simulate driving or flying.

Understand headings, subheadings and points 2

This worksheet accompanies **p.18–21** in the *Level 1 Skills Book*

Name ______________________ Date __________

1 Skim read the article about computer games.

2 Now draw a line to match the paragraph numbers on the left with an appropriate heading from the list on the right.

Paragraphs	Headings
Paragraph 1	Be a hero for a day
Paragraph 2	Couch potato or Coach Potato?
Paragraph 3	Control a nation or fly a fighter
Paragraph 4	A game for everyone

1 There are many kinds of computer games available nowadays. Times have moved on since the arcade games of the 1970s and 1980s. Today's computer game player has a huge range of games from which to choose. Since video games became popular in the 1970s, manufacturers have created games to suit everybody's need.

2 One of the most popular computer game types, or 'genres', is the role-playing game. In this type of game, you play as if you are a particular character. The character you choose to play will have a range of skills depending on what type of person they are. For instance, they might be better at weapons mastery or at stealth. In these games, the objective is to complete an adventure or quest.

3 Another type of game that's popular is a sports-based game. These cover any type of sport that you might imagine, such as football and rugby. If there's a particular sport you enjoy, you can guarantee there's a game based on it. You can either play a game where you are the team coach, which is a strategy-based game, or you can play a game where you are one of the players, known as 'electronic sports' because you are playing as if you are one of the players.

4 Simulation games are also very popular. These are games that allow you to see how situations would develop over time. In games like this, you start off some kind of situation or create a business and develop it through history. You can build families, cities, businesses, hospitals, theme parks or even whole nations. Some simulation games are known as 'strategy games' where you play out situations like battles. Simulation games also cover games where you can simulate driving or flying.

B3 Organise a text 1

This worksheet accompanies **p.18–21** in the *Level 1 Skills Book*

Name ______________________ Date __________

1 Read these four paragraphs about a particular type of computer game: strategy games.

2 Decide in which order you think the paragraphs should be placed.

____

3 Write the reasons for your decision under each paragraph.

A

A major type of strategy game is the 'grand strategy game' where you can act out scenarios from history and see what would happen if you were in charge. Some games let you play a leading role in battles, or play out events in history. You might choose to be Julius Caesar and see how his armies would have got on under your control, or you might choose to be a battlefield commander in World War II. Some 'grand strategy games' also let you play out situations that are fictitious, such as futuristic battles or battles involving magical skills.

____

____

B

If you really like playing as if you are in charge of everything, you might like other strategy games where you get to oversee the developments of a family, community, city or nation. In these games, you don't play a particular role, and you might not have particular qualities as a leader, but you make choices that affect the lives of the creatures over which you have control. In these types of game, you realise that the choices that you make have an impact on the lives of your citizens, and not always in ways you might expect. In all strategy games, you need to make choices about your actions, and you have to face the consequences – good or bad.

____

____

C

Strategy games are part of a category of games known as 'simulations'. 'Simulation' means 'imitating' or 'acting out'. It can also mean 'representing something in real life in a virtual environment'. Strategy games model what might happen in a situation if you were in charge of making the decisions!

____

____

D

Another type of fictitious strategy game is sometimes known as a 'nation simulation' game. This is where you choose to play a particular leader of a particular nation, and see how the nation would get on under your leadership. You could choose to play as if you are Attila the Hun, Abraham Lincoln or even a Greek god! These are different from 'grand strategy games' because you might not necessarily be involved in a battle, and you will probably need to use a range of other skills, like negotiation.

____

____

Literacy Teacher's Handbook Level 1 © Edexcel Limited 2006

B4 Organise a text 2

This worksheet accompanies **p.18–21** in the *Level 1 Skills Book*

Name ______________________ Date ____________

1 These directions to a train station are out of order. Work out the right order and number them 1–5.

2 Then underline or highlight the words that helped you put the sentences in order.

Getting from Manchester Victoria train station to Manchester Piccadilly train station:

At the main junction, you will see pedestrian signs pointing to Piccadilly Station. Keep going straight on. You will see Malmaison Hotel on your right. Once you pass Malmaison Hotel, follow the fork in the road up the incline to Piccadilly Station's entrance.

First, come out of the train station through the main exit opposite the Metrolink platform. You should be facing a road with a taxi rank and several bus stops. Urbis information centre is in front of you.

When you get to The Triangle, you will see the giant TV screen on your right, and the Arndale Centre tower on your left. Selfridges is in front of you, with the giant windmills. Go up between the Arndale and Selfridges, following the road towards Marks & Spencer.

Once you are facing Urbis, go left up to the top of the road, and then turn right, so you are walking alongside the museum. You will see the Printworks on your left hand side and The Triangle in front of you.

When you get to Marks & Spencer, turn left, go underneath the Arndale food court, which is overhead, and continue up Market Street. Keep going up here until you get to Debenhams. Then go past Debenhams. Piccadilly Bus Station should be on your right. Keep going up to the main junction.

B5 Make sense of an image

This worksheet accompanies **p.28–29** in the *Level 1 Skills Book*

Name ______________________ Date ____________

Computer games often have symbols on the packaging that help you understand what is in the content, or who the manufacturers intend the audience to be.

1 Match the symbol on the left with the definition on the right.

2 Then decide whether the symbol is giving you a clue about content or audience by adding 'C' (for content) or 'A' (for audience) in the final column.

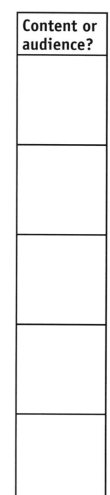

Symbol	Definition	Content or audience?
7+ www.pegi.info	Contains acts of violence	
	Suitable for people over 7 years of age	
16+ www.pegi.info	Contains bad language	
	Suitable for people over 16 years of age	
@*!	Contains material some people may find frightening	

Literacy Teacher's Handbook Level 1 © Edexcel Limited 2006

Understand headings, subheadings and points 3

This worksheet accompanies **p.18–21** in the *Level 1 Skills Book*

Name ____________________ Date __________

When we design informative posters, we arrange the information in order of how important it is. For example, you would not expect to find a phone number to buy tickets for an event before the rest of the information about the event, because you need to know what the event is before you phone for tickets.

1 You have been asked to design an informative poster advertising a karting morning for people where you work. Read the items of information about the event and decide the order in which you think they should be placed on the page. Put a number from 1 to 12 in the box by each item to show the order.

2 On another sheet of paper, create a poster advertising the event, putting the most important information at the top and working your way down to the least important information at the bottom.

3 You might want to use other features such as bold text or underlining to help the reader find key information quickly. You could also add images to help the reader understand the information more easily.

Item	Order
Springtown's kart course is on Town Road. Head out of the town centre, go past the supermarket on the left, go over the next roundabout and the kart course is on the right.	☐
Be there for 9:00 a.m. if you want to take part.	☐
Car parking is free.	☐
This will be held at Springtown's kart course.	☐
Entry is free for employees.	☐
You will need a £1 to operate the lockers.	☐
All employees are invited to a Karting morning.	☐
All equipment is provided.	☐
The karting morning will take place on 18th May.	☐
Following the races at 11:30 a.m., employees are welcome to stay to eat in the cafeteria.	☐
The cafeteria is open from 12:30 until 2:00 p.m.	☐
You don't need to have done karting before because there will be practice laps.	☐

C Understanding what writers want their readers to do

(pages 32–47 in the Skills Book)

Speaking and Listening	Reading	Writing
SLc/L1.1 Speak clearly in a way which suits the situation. ***SLlr/L1.2*** Listen for and understand explanations, instructions and narratives on different topics in a range of contexts.	***Rt/L1.2*** Recognise how language and other textual features are used to achieve different purposes, e.g. *to instruct, explain, describe, persuade*. ***Rw/L1.2*** Recognise and understand the vocabulary associated with different types of text, using appropriate strategies to work out meaning.	***Wt/L1.3*** Present information in a logical sequence, using paragraphs where appropriate. ***Wt/L1.4*** Use language suitable for purpose and audience.

Coverage of standards

The chart above lists coverage of standards in Section C of the Level 1 Skills Book. It also lists additional standards that could be taught with this section, using the suggestions below.

Section outline

Section C covers how writers achieve their purpose. It requires students to consider what the writer wants the reader to think or do, and how they have constructed the text so that their purposes can be achieved.

The skills covered are:

- recognise the purpose of a text
- understand how writers use words and features in informative, explanatory, descriptive or persuasive writing.

Approaches to teaching

Two important concepts need to be taught in this section:

- what writers may want the reader to think or do as a result of reading their text
- how writing within a particular non-fiction text type shares common features with other writing of a similar text type.

Students need to have the skills to recognise the writer's aims and purposes, showing understanding of the key features of various types of writing, and how they differ. They should have an awareness of the way words and sentences differ in informative, explanatory, descriptive or persuasive writing. They should also show an understanding of how the layout of a text can inform the reader of its purpose. When considering layout, students should think about the way structure and sequence can reveal the writer's purpose.

When studying purpose, students should be taught to explore the way verb types and tenses are associated with particular purposes, such as the use of present tense in informative or explanatory text, or the use of verbs as commands in instructive text. Students should also explore the way a writer uses adjectives for different purposes in different types of writing, such as the use of adjectives to persuade a reader, or to clarify an unfamiliar topic in informative writing.

Linked Speaking and Listening and Writing activities

This section will give you the opportunity to target relevant Speaking and Listening and Writing standards through activities such as those that follow.

Speaking and Listening

- *Paired work.* The pair should sit back-to-back. Give one student a piece of paper with a simple mathematical shape on it. The other should have a blank piece of paper and a pencil. The student with the image should describe the shape to their partner without looking at the image that their partner is creating. Give students a short time limit and then compare the illustrations *(SLc/L1.1)*.

- *Paired work.* Show students several short clips from a range of television programmes, including persuasive adverts, explanatory programmes, infomercials, cookery programmes and sports reportage. Ask students to work in pairs to decide which text type each example corresponds to. They may find that some examples fit into more than one category *(SLlr/L1.2)*.

Writing

- Ask students to consider a process or activity that they regularly undertake. This should ideally be something with which other students are unfamiliar. The student should construct a set of instructions for that process or activity, using all the appropriate stylistic features of the text type, including second person address and an imperative tone. They could also include diagrams or illustrations *(Wt/L1.3)*.
- Give students a short piece of text that has been written for an adult audience. This could be informative, instructive or explanatory. Students should highlight words and phrases that will need simplification for a younger audience, rewriting the text as appropriate. If students have access to word processing facilities they will be able to edit the text with more ease. Students should highlight their alterations and annotate them to explain the thinking behind the changes they have made *(Wt/L1.4)*.

Photocopiable worksheets

The following photocopiable sheets are included for Section C:

C1 Recognise the purpose of a text 1

C2 Recognise the purpose of a text 2

C3 Understand the way words are used in instructions

C4 How words are used in descriptions

C5 How words are used in explanations

C6 How words are used in persuasive texts.

C1 Recognise the purpose of a text 1

This worksheet accompanies **p.32–33** in the *Level 1 Skills Book*

Name ______________________________ Date ____________

1 Draw a line to match the text types on the left to the sentences on the right.

2 In each box on the right, highlight the words that show you what text type it is.

3 Now choose one of the text types (persuasive, descriptive, informative, instructive and explanatory). Write your own sentence to fit the text type.

Text type		Sentence
Persuasive		Before you switch the kettle on, fill it with water. Then you will need to press down the switch until it switches itself off or the water boils. ____________________ ____________________
Descriptive		£1 a week means a huge amount to an abandoned dog like me. Your gift will help The Dogs' Trust give us all the love and support we need. ____________________ ____________________
Informative		Volcanoes erupt because of movements in the Earth's surface. When pieces of the Earth's surface (known as plates) move, magma from below the surface is forced up along the edge of the plate. ____________________ ____________________
Instructive		The house is a four-bed semi-detached, occupying a position at the end of a large driveway. There is a large, well-maintained garden to the front, and the garden to the rear has spectacular views of the Lake District. ____________________ ____________________
Explanatory		Swimming is a good activity for all-round cardio-vascular fitness. It exercises your lungs as well as your body. ____________________ ____________________

Literacy Teacher's Handbook Level 1 © Edexcel Limited 2006

C2 Recognise the purpose of a text 2

This worksheet accompanies **p.32–41** in the *Level 1 Skills Book*

Name ______________________ Date __________

1 Collect a range of non-fiction texts that cover the text types you have been exploring: informative, explanatory, persuasive, instructive and descriptive. Some suggestions for the kind of texts you might find are in the table below.

2 Then complete the table and explain why your examples match each particular text type.

Informative	**Explanatory**	**Persuasive**
Suggested example: *tourist guide to a town* Your example:	Suggested example: *a magazine article* Your example:	Suggested example: *an advert or letter* Your example:
I know this is informative because...	I know this is explanatory because...	I know this is persuasive because...

Instructive	**Descriptive**
Suggested example: *a recipe or manual* Your example:	Suggested example: *a holiday brochure* Your example:
I know this is instructive because...	I know this is descriptive because...

C3 Understand the way words are used in instructions

This worksheet accompanies **p.34–35** in the *Level 1 Skills Book*

Name ______________________ Date __________

1 Read the instructions below for making a cup of tea.

2 Fill in each gap with one of these words.

when	then	finally	after

3 Then underline all the verbs that are a command, such as *stir* and *fill*.

How to make the perfect cup of tea

Materials and equipment:

- a kettle
- a cup or mug
- a teaspoon
- a tea bag
- milk
- sugar

1. Before you switch the kettle on, fill it with water. __________ you will need to press the switch so that the water boils. If you are using a kettle on a gas hob, take it off the gas burner when there is a steady whistle.

2. __________ the kettle is boiling, prepare the cup by placing the tea bag in it.
Then add the boiling water to the cup, taking care not to overfill it. Leave the tea for up to five minutes, depending on the strength you require. If you want a weaker cup of tea, remove the teabag __________ a minute. If you prefer a stronger cup of tea, leave the teabag for the full amount of time.

3. __________ add milk and sugar as desired and stir.

Literacy Teacher's Handbook Level 1 © Edexcel Limited 2006

C4 How words are used in descriptions

This worksheet accompanies **p.36–37** in the *Level 1 Skills Book*

Name ______________________ Date __________

In descriptive texts, words are used to help clarify what something or someone looks like, so a reader can imagine it.

1 Look at this illustration of a house and its floor plan.

2 Complete the description of the house with appropriate adjectives. The first has been done for you.

This is a *semi-detached* house situated in a/an ____________ area. It has a/an ____________ garage. There are ____________ gardens and a/an ____________ greenhouse. There is a/an ____________ entrance hall, a/an ____________ cloakroom and a/an ____________ lounge/ dining area. The kitchen is ____________ and ____________. Upstairs, there are ____________ bedrooms. The ____________ bedroom has a/an ____________ bathroom. The other bedrooms share a/an ____________ bathroom, which has a/an ____________ bath and ____________ shower. The house is centrally-heated, but also has ____________ gas fires and ____________ water heating.

How words are used in explanations

This worksheet accompanies **p.38–39** in the *Level 1 Skills Book*

Name ______________________________ Date ____________

An explanatory text tells **how** or **why** something happens. Explanatory writing includes lots of connectives that help explain a process.

This explanation about volcanoes has connectives missing. Add the right connectives from the list below. Try to use all the connectives in the list. You will need to use some of them more than once.

therefore because as a result so which

Volcanoes are hills or mountains made of lava ______________ comes from below the surface of the Earth. When volcanoes erupt, lava and ash build up and ______________ a cone shaped hill is formed. A great deal of heat is created when a volcano erupts, and ______________ some volcanoes give off clouds of ash and gas. Other volcanoes produce red-hot streams of lava ______________ run down their sides. Volcanoes can be formed in the sea as well as on land. Undersea volcanoes sometimes grow very high, ______________ their tops reach above the sea level, and ______________ they form islands.

Volcanoes can cause a great deal of damage, ______________ the gas and lava they produce can injure and kill people and animals, and destroy crops and buildings. ______________, when people who live near a volcano get warning that it is about to erupt, they often move away ______________ they can avoid danger.

Literacy Teacher's Handbook Level 1 © Edexcel Limited 2006

C6 How words are used in persuasive texts

This worksheet accompanies **p.40–41** in the *Level 1 Skills Book*

Name ______________________ Date __________

Persuasive texts are texts that want you to do something – for example, buy something, change your behaviour or just agree with the author. Some ways they do this include:

- giving lots of *reasons* to make you want to do something
- giving the writer's *opinions*
- appealing to your *feelings* (so you feel bad if you don't do what the text says, or feel good if you do)
- using lots of *different types of print* (**bold**, *italics*, colour, etc.).

1 Read through the persuasive text below. Some words or phrases have been underlined. Look at each underlined word or phrase in turn and decide which of the four methods is being used:

- reason
- opinion
- feeling
- type of print

More than one method may be used at one time. Write the feature(s) alongside the word or phrase. The first example has been done for you.

The Intellicise Rowing Machine

Use of big bold print.

Unbeatable power – unbeatable performance!

The new Intellicise Rowing Machine is such a fantastic way to exercise. For all-round, total fitness, **nothing beats the Intellicise**!

- Exercise *all major muscle groups*
- *Impact free* so there's less chance of injury
- *Easy to install* – fits into the smallest room
- Program to your *own fitness level*
- When combined with a carefully controlled diet, a great way to *lose weight*

Feeling unfit? Banish those extra pounds and discover your own inner fitness. You'll feel better in body and mind!

Spelling words correctly

(pages 48–59 in the Skills Book)

Speaking and Listening	Reading	Writing
SLlr/L1.4 Provide feedback and confirmation when listening to others.	***Rw/L1.3*** Recognise and understand an increasing range of vocabulary, applying knowledge of word structure, related words, word roots, derivations, borrowings.	***Ww/L1.1*** Spell correctly words used most often in work, studies and daily life.

Coverage of standards

The chart above lists coverage of standards in Section D of the Level 1 Skills Book. It also lists additional standards that could be taught with this section, using the suggestions below.

Section outline

Section D covers spelling. It requires students to be able to recognise common errors in familiar spelling patterns. The materials cover a range of techniques to help learn common spelling patterns.

Approaches to teaching

Students need to appreciate the need for accurate spelling and to understand that their own spelling is, in all likelihood, more accurate than they may perceive.

At this level, students need to be able to spell familiar words correctly and access a range of strategies to help them internalise any less familiar spellings they come across.

They need strategies to help them remember more complex patterns for polysyllabic words, and to help them remember unusual words. Students should also become more accurate in identifying errors in basic spelling, or in familiar, less complex patterns in polysyllabic words.

Commonly used spelling strategies

These include:

- sounding it out (both individual letters and as syllable blocks)
- taking off the affixes and suffixes to spell the root of the word correctly
- using a mnemonic, e.g. big elephants can't always use small escalators – *because*
- thinking of other words that have the same pattern or belong to the same word family
- looking for words within words, e.g. *separate* contains *a rat*
- learning by sight, e.g. look–cover–write–check, and learning by hand memory (i.e. repeating the movement of writing the word until the hand muscles 'remember' how to write it)
- visual memory, e.g. *b-e-d* helps students who mix up *b* and *d* because it reminds them that the stems of the letters are on the outside, like bedposts.

Linked Speaking and Listening and Writing activities

This section will give you the opportunity to target relevant Speaking and Listening and Writing standards through activities such as those that follow.

Speaking and Listening

- *Paired work.* Students sound out problematic words to one another, stressing and emphasising the letters or syllables within the word, while their partner writes the word, aiming for the correct spelling *(SLlr/L1.4)*.
- *Paired work.* Students should use their own writing to identify one or more familiar words that are problematic in spelling. Working with a partner, they should then swap lists of problematic vocabulary and design a cheat sheet to help their partners remember their spellings.

Writing

- Read through a piece of text with a given number of basic errors. Tell students the number of errors and then ask them to highlight these, adding corrections alongside the original mistakes *(Ww/L1.1)*.
- Ask students to bring in a piece of their own writing. Ask them to estimate the percentage of errors they might have made, for example, 50 per cent. They should count 100 words and then highlight any words that they think may not be accurate. Students may wish to colour-code their words, highlighting 'definitely correct' words in green, 'possibly incorrect' words in orange and 'definitely incorrect' words in pink. They can then check and correct their errors. They may be pleasantly surprised because they get fewer words wrong than they think. *(Ww/L1.1)*.
- Give students a short piece of accurately-spelled text, and ask them to highlight familiar words with which writers may have problems. You may wish to give students patterns or word families where writers frequently have problems, such as particular vowel blends, like ai or a_e, and ask them to identify all the words that fit the pattern. They should then create a table of their findings, putting words into categories of spelling. When they have completed this, you could ask them to design a poster or a short piece of writing that illustrates all the words with one of the patterns. For example, a poster demonstrating all words with i_e might include a *white* car, an apple with a *bite* out of it and a *kite (Ww/L1.1)*.
- Give students a bank of commonly misspelled familiar words such as that below. Ask students to design a series of images, advice or mnemonics to help others remember how to spell each word *(Ww/L1.1)*.

Spelling challenge!

Here are 50 words your students could check they know how to spell.

Literacy	Numeracy	ICT	Humanities	Science
Comma	Mathematics	Computer	Cause	Biology
Sentence	Sum	Printer	Citizen	Chemistry
Spelling	Zero	Scanner	Desert	Physics
Punctuation	Length	Browser	Iceburg	Watt
Grammar	Depth	Monitor	Weather	Acid
Question	Width	Function	Secondary	Heart
Summary	Factor	Menu	Saviour	Vein
Speech	Equal	Design	Belief	Artery
Draft	Value	Format	Ocean	Energy
Phrase	Metre	Preview	Atlas	Material

Photocopiable worksheets

The following photocopiable sheets are included for Section D:

D1 Commonly used words 1

D2 Commonly used words 2

D3 Spelling plurals

D4 Mnemonics

D5 Homophones

D6 Spelling tricks.

D1 Commonly used words 1

This worksheet accompanies **p.48–51** in the *Level 1 Skills Book*

Name ______________________ Date __________

1 There are five spelling mistakes in each of the texts below. Find and underline them.

2 Then work out the type of words each writer has a problem with and write down the letters that the writer is getting confused. For example: It was <u>tuff</u> to say that he couldn't borrow my <u>stough</u> but it was late and I'd had <u>enuff</u>. Mistake pattern: <u>uff, ough</u>.

A

I was going strate to the barbecue with my mayte. We were in a hurry because I didn't want to be lait. If we weren't on time I wasn't going to get a plait of my favourite barbecue chicken. I took a caik that I'd cooked earlier.

Mistake pattern: __________

B

I wanted to meat outside the cinema but my friend was kean to meat inside. She wanted to get there early so she could buy some sweats and then get a good seet.

Mistake pattern: __________

C

Even though it was nearly nite, it was still very brite outside. The sky was clear and there was only a small whight cloud on the horizon. Since it was lite I sat in the garden to wright a letter to my friend.

Mistake pattern: __________

D

It was with some releif that I realised my freind was on time. I beleived she would be late since she has a memory like a seive, but she arrived on time, thanks to a reminder she recieved.

Mistake pattern: __________

Literacy Teacher's Handbook Level 1 © Edexcel Limited 2006

D2 Commonly used words 2

This worksheet accompanies **p.48–51** in the *Level 1 Skills Book*

Name ______________________ Date ____________

1 Cut up the cards below and sort them into piles, grouping words with the same patterns together. For instance *whale* and *cake* might go in the same pile, as they both have a_e patterns.

2 Now sort the words into rhyming patterns, for instance *straight* and *eight*. Which words have the same sounds but different letter patterns? Can you add any more words to this list?

mate	wait	eight	fail
whale	late	day	snail
train	same	change	spare
care	hair	brain	bake
dare	cake	air	bear
bait	chair	share	date
stay	fare	straight	Spain
main	fair	lane	may

D3 Spelling plurals

This worksheet accompanies **p.48–51** in the *Level 1 Skills Book*

Name ______________________ Date __________

One common pattern that confuses writers is the plural of -y words like *lady* and *party*. One way of remembering whether an ending becomes -ys or -ies is to look at the letter before the -y.

- If it is a vowel, you keep -ys (so *toy* becomes *toys*).
- If it is a consonant, you need to replace the -y with -ies (so *party* becomes *parties*).

1 Look at the words below and decide whether they take a -ys or an -ies ending. Circle the words that change to -ies.

boy	jelly	try	lady
baby	key	way	spy
penny	fly	puppy	guy
city	pony	bully	survey

2 Nouns that end in -ch, -sh, -s, -x and -z take -es and not just -s in the plural (so *bench* becomes *benches* and *pass* becomes *passes*).

Circle all the words in the table below that need -es plurals.

3 You should also be able to find a matching word for each word you have highlighted that needs -es. For instance, *fox* and *box* both end in -x. Draw lines to link these word pairs.

dish	bus	table	kiss
coach	gas	box	peach
dot	cat	dribble	church
fox	lunch	wish	cross

Literacy Teacher's Handbook Level 1 © Edexcel Limited 2006

D4 Mnemonics

This worksheet accompanies **p.48–51** in the *Level 1 Skills Book*

Name ______________________ Date __________

Mnemonics are ways of remembering how to spell difficult words. They can help you remember tricky letter combinations or a whole word.

- You can use visual reminders, like a shirt with *one* **c**ollar and *two* **s**leeves for *necessary*.
- Or you can think of words within words, like *a rat* in *separate*.
- You can also use acrostics, where the first letter of each word in an easily-remembered phrase stands for each letter in a difficult word, like *big elephants can't always use small escalators* for *because*. It can also be helpful to picture an acrostic in your mind.

Look at the words in the table below. What mnemonics might you use to help you remember how to spell them? Add a picture, acrostic, words within words or another type of reminder next to each word.

geography	
arithmetic	
rhythm	
business	
parliament	

D5 Homophones

This worksheet accompanies **p.54–55** in the *Level 1 Skills Book*

Name ______________________ Date __________

to/too/two

1 Match the definition on the right with the correct spelling on the left.

two
too
to

also, as well, a lot or very
part of an action, or shows where someone went
a number

2 Read the sentence below and put the right *to/too/two* in the space provided.

I was going ______ the shops ______ get a couple of pints of milk for breakfast the next morning. I went ______ the fridge and picked up ______ pints of milk. Then I thought I might want some juice to go with breakfast, so I picked up a carton of fresh juice ______.

"Is that all?" asked the shopkeeper when I got ______ the check-out.

"Can I have a bar of chocolate ______?" I said, then I remembered my sister. "Better make that ______," I said. I hate it when she pinches mine.

"One for your sister, ______?" the shopkeeper asked, with a smile.

"You bet," I said, then left the shop ______ go home.

Literacy Teacher's Handbook Level 1 © Edexcel Limited 2006

D6 Spelling tricks

This worksheet accompanies **p.48–57** in the *Level 1 Skills Book*

Name ______________________ Date ____________

1 See if you can think of some ways to remember how to spell the tricky words below. You might want to use 'look-cover-write-check' or write the word in large letters, then trace it with your finger. Or you might also want to think of a mnemonic to help you remember it, such as a visual image or an acrostic.

2 Alongside the word, write down the method you used to help you remember how to spell it.

Tricky word	Method of remembering it
sincerely	
business	
explanation	
autumn	
necessary	
outrageous	
miscellaneous	
technique	
technology	
physical	

E Punctuation

(pages 60–69 in the Skills Book)

Speaking and Listening	Reading	Writing
SLc/L1.4 Provide feedback and confirmation when listening to others.	***Rs/L1.2*** Use punctuation to help their understanding.	***Wt/L1.6*** Proof-read and revise writing for accuracy and meaning. ***Ws/L1.3*** Punctuate sentences correctly and use punctuation so that meaning is clear. ***Ws/L1.1*** Write in complete sentences.

Coverage of standards

The chart above lists coverage of Level 1 standards in Section E of the Skills Book. It also lists additional standards that could be taught with this section, using the suggestions below.

Section outline

Section E covers punctuation. It requires students to be able to demarcate their sentences appropriately, using a range of punctuation to denote the ending of a sentence. In this way, it is also important for students to understand the mechanics and grammar of a sentence.

Students are shown how to use the following punctuation marks:

- capital letters
- full stops
- question marks
- exclamation marks.

Approaches to teaching

Students need to consider the grammar of a sentence and be able to punctuate the boundaries of sentences accurately. They will benefit from exploring what features make an accurate sentence and they will need to be reminded of the ways in which they may end a sentence. Some students may need reminding about connective splicing, where they join sentences together with a row of simple connectives, like *and* or *so*. Other students may incorrectly use commas to splice sentences together, using a comma instead of a full stop. They will need practice putting the right punctuation into their own writing.

Whole class tip

Activities where students practise identifying mistakes and inserting the right punctuation will be useful. Paired work, with students working as far as possible with a partner of the same level of skill, will also help students discuss and internalise the processes of punctuating sentences. Reading aloud is a good way for a less confident writer to identify where punctuation breaks should go, especially if they work with a partner.

Linked Speaking and Listening and Writing activities

This section will give you the opportunity to target relevant Speaking and Listening and Writing standards through activities such as those that follow.

Speaking and Listening

- *Paired work.* Ask students to read an unpunctuated passage aloud to a partner. They should agree where the punctuation should go and what kind of punctuation is needed.

Writing

- *Paired work.* Ask students to bring in a piece of their own writing and check that they have punctuated it accurately by reading it aloud to a partner. They should notice if they overuse simple connectives, if they use a comma instead of a full stop and if they use the right punctuation at the end of their sentence. Having done this, students should set themselves a personal target for sentence punctuation *(Wt/L1.6)*.

- Give students a passage of unpunctuated writing. Omit all of the full stops, question marks and exclamation marks, and then ask students to decide which pieces of punctuation should be used, and where they should be placed *(Ws/L1.3)*.
- Use a word processing package that can recognise sentence fragments. Ask students to write five sentences that do not have all the necessary grammatical features of a sentence. Then ask them to write five grammatically accurate sentences and add these. They should use the grammar checker on the word processing software to check whether their sentences are fragments or not. They may then wish to add words to the sentence fragments until they are grammatically secure. For example, the fragment *Bolton Wanderers' star player* could become *Bolton Wanderers' star player is injured (Ws/L1.1)*.

Photocopiable worksheets

The following photocopiable sheets are included for Section E:

E1 Capital letters 1

E2 Capital letters 2

E3 Capital letters 3

E4 Full stops

E5 Sentences and sentence fragments 1

E6 Sentences and sentence fragments 2.

E1 Capital letters 1

This worksheet accompanies **p.60–61** in the *Level 1 Skills Book*

Name ______________________ Date ____________

Remember that capitals are used:

- for names
- for places
- for months
- for days of the week
- at the beginning of sentences.

1 Read the e-mail below. Some words that may need capital letters have been underlined. Write in the capital letters where they need to go. Watch out – not all the underlined words need capital letters.

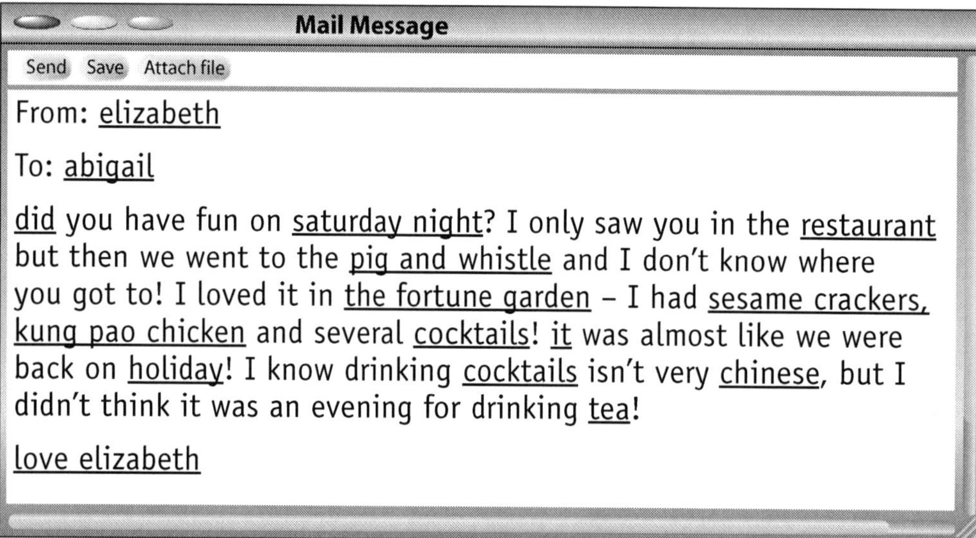

Mail Message

Send Save Attach file

From: elizabeth

To: abigail

did you have fun on saturday night? I only saw you in the restaurant but then we went to the pig and whistle and I don't know where you got to! I loved it in the fortune garden – I had sesame crackers, kung pao chicken and several cocktails! it was almost like we were back on holiday! I know drinking cocktails isn't very chinese, but I didn't think it was an evening for drinking tea!

love elizabeth

2 Look at the reply to the e-mail. Tick the underlined words where capitals are needed and put a cross next to words that need to stay in lower case.

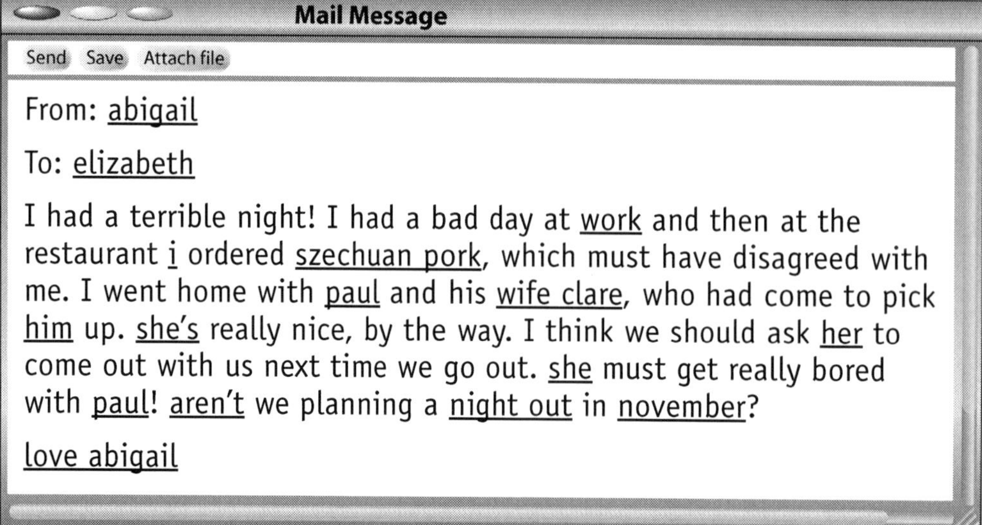

Mail Message

Send Save Attach file

From: abigail

To: elizabeth

I had a terrible night! I had a bad day at work and then at the restaurant i ordered szechuan pork, which must have disagreed with me. I went home with paul and his wife clare, who had come to pick him up. she's really nice, by the way. I think we should ask her to come out with us next time we go out. she must get really bored with paul! aren't we planning a night out in november?

love abigail

Literacy Teacher's Handbook Level 1 © Edexcel Limited 2006

E2 Capital letters 2

This worksheet accompanies **p.62–63** in the *Level 1 Skills Book*

Name ________________________ Date ____________

1 Read the letter below. The writer has made several errors with his capital letters.

2 Underline the incorrect capitals in one colour, then use another colour to underline the words that have lower case letters but need capitals.

6 riversway terrace
hazelton
gloucestershire
GL41 7RG

discount holidays
oxford road
swindon
Wiltshire
WL2 3EQ

monday, 21 november

dear sir Or madam

I am Writing to say how Disappointed I am with my recent Holiday with discount holidays. I expect a Full Refund for the reasons I will Outline below.

firstly, the room was in a Dreadful State when we arrived. the maid had not finished cleaning, and there was dust everywhere, including on the Television Set. it was Filthy and my Wife was Disgusted. secondly, the Breakfast was not up to my Usual Standards. there was no Tomato served with the English Breakfast and I was disappointed by the Fried Bread and Mushrooms. At Night, there was a Very Loud Disco that played Terrible pop music. I could Barely Sleep. We expect a Full Refund.

Yours Sincerely

Mr B Booth

E3 Capital letters 3

This worksheet accompanies **p.60–61** in the *Level 1 Skills Book*

Name ______________________ Date __________

Capital letters are used for **languages** but not for other subjects taught in school. For example, mathematics is written in lower case letters, but English has a capital letter.

Historical periods and **events**, such as *the Industrial Revolution*, have capital letters.

Nationalities and **cultures** have capital letters, e.g. *Irish, Muslim*.

Main words in **book and film titles** also have capital letters, e.g. *Harry Potter and the Order of the Phoenix*.

Read the text below and circle where capital letters should go. You should find 28.

I enjoyed doing history at school. I particularly enjoyed studying the vikings and the middle ages. I wasn't so keen on reading about victorian england or the industrial revolution. I also liked learning languages, and I really enjoyed french, even though the teacher, mr cannon, had a very odd french accent. He sounded more welsh than french to me! I really wish I'd had the chance to do spanish or portuguese, but these weren't taught at our school. I liked some bits of maths, but I found algebra the hardest. I preferred shapes and area rather than working out calculations. My worst bit of maths was graph work, because I was really messy at drawing them.

My favourite subject was art. I really liked all the practical work we did, but I also liked looking at other people's artwork. I really like georgia o'keeffe, but I also like artists like monet and renoir. English was okay. I enjoyed reading *of mice and men* and I thought the film was really good. We also watched the film of *all my sons* but I didn't enjoy it as much.

Literacy Teacher's Handbook Level 1 © Edexcel Limited 2006

E4 Full stops

This worksheet accompanies **p.62–65** in the *Level 1 Skills Book*

Name ______________________ Date ____________

One mistake that many writers make is to use words such as *and, so* and *because* too often in their writing to join together sentences that really need a full stop.

Read the following article aloud. As you read, circle any places where you need a full stop rather than a connective. The first one has been done for you.

A teenager has been banned from roaming the streets at night. Ashley Whiteside, 17, has been causing disruption around the streets of Hammersham every evening for the last four months, ever since he moved to the area (and) he has been charged with several counts of drunken behaviour because he was seen drinking alcohol in the streets on numerous occasions and riding a motorbike while under the influence so he was charged with drunk and disorderly behaviour earlier today at Hammersham County Court and as a result the judge issued an Anti-Social Behaviour Order banning Ashley from the streets so his mother said, "I am really disappointed in Ashley but I don't know what to do with him and I can't stop him going out on the streets every night because he just laughs at me so I hope this has taught him a lesson so he realises how serious all this is."

Ashley has also been banned from driving for 18 months because he was caught riding his motorbike while under the influence of alcohol so he also received a fine and he will have to retake his driver's test when the full period is up and he will also need to attend a series of alcohol abuse clinics to get his drinking under control.

E5 Sentences and sentence fragments 1

This worksheet accompanies **p.64–65** in the *Level 1 Skills Book*

Name ______________________ Date __________

A piece of writing needs three things in order to be a sentence:

- it has to make sense on its own
- it must have a verb (an action word)
- it has to have a capital letter and a full stop.

All sentences include these features. Some writers use parts of a sentence by mistake, putting a full stop in where it is not needed. This is called a sentence fragment. It is a grammatical error.

Look at the following sentences and sentence fragments. Write 'S' in the boxes that have full sentences and 'SF' in the boxes that have a sentence fragment. The first two have been done for you.

He was acting like a baby. S	Crying over spilt milk. SF
Alison has blonde hair.	The hair products were on special offer.
The hair products.	Basil sat down.
Opening the door.	The door opened.
Free strawberries.	Get free strawberries when you buy a pot of cream.
Now on sale.	Buy it today.
I always recycle my newspapers.	Bottles and jars too.
When you get to Reading.	You need to take the M4.
You look really cool.	In that jacket.

Literacy Teacher's Handbook Level 1 © Edexcel Limited 2006

E6 Sentences and sentence fragments 2

This worksheet accompanies **p.62–65** in the *Level 1 Skills Book*

Name ______________________ Date __________

Make these sentence fragments into full sentences by adding some more information to them. Don't forget the full stop at the end.

1 As the referee blew his whistle ______________________

____

2 Accelerating to full speed ______________________

____

3 Capital letters ______________________

____

4 On hot days ______________________

____

5 Missing the bus ______________________

____

6 Growing up ______________________

____

7 Work the television remote ______________________

____

8 Musicians gather ______________________

____

9 Feed cats ______________________

____

10 Refrigerators ______________________

____

Using good grammar

(pages 70–75 in the Skills Book)

Speaking and Listening	Reading	Writing
SLlr/L1.5 Make contributions relevant to the situation and the subject.	***Rs/L1.1*** Use implicit and explicit grammatical knowledge e.g. of different sentence forms, types of word, verb tense, word order along with own knowledge and experience to predict meaning, try out plausible meanings, and to read and check for sense.	***Ws/L1.2*** Use correct grammar e.g. subject-verb agreement, correct use of tense. ***Wt/L1.6*** Proof-read and revise writing for accuracy and meaning.

Coverage of standards

The chart above lists coverage of standards in Section F of the Level 1 Skills Book. It also lists additional standards that could be taught with this section, using the suggestions below.

Section outline

Section F covers grammatical features of writing. It requires students to be able to build on the work in Section E, by considering other features of a sentence, and other rules of language that help make sentences accurate. You may find that pupils who speak English as an additional language need more support in this section.

The following skills are covered:

- subject-verb agreement
- using the correct tense
- use of *to have* and *to be.*

Approaches to teaching

Students may find that they make mistakes in writing as a result of inappropriate transference of spoken language patterns into their writing. Because of newer, less formal language styles, such as text messaging or instant messaging, students may find that they are prone to informal styles and abbreviations that are inappropriate for more formal types of writing. It may help to explore with students the main differences between spoken and written English, and informal and formal styles of writing, alongside a reinforcement of the rules of written English that require more formality. It would be of particular use to explore the levels of formality in the types of transactional writing students will be most likely to encounter outside the educational environment, including e-mail messages and letters.

When reading, it may be useful to explore the ways in which writing can become more formal by changing some of the language, for example, taking an informal letter or message and translating it into something more formal.

Whole class tip

Rank ordering activities, where students are given a range of texts to order in terms of formality, would help students understand the features of language that contribute to formality, undertaking an investigation of language within writing.

Another approach that may help students make the leap from spoken style to accurate written grammar is to create a bank of common spoken words and phrases that are inappropriate in written language. For example, 'I were going' is a common spoken grammatical error that sometimes migrates into written language. Students should be aware that the way they speak can affect the way they write and spell. An example of a common mistake is the use of 'could of' instead of 'could have' or 'could've', again imported from spoken English.

For students with English as an additional or second language, grammatical errors often manifest themselves in verb-subject disagreement, for example, 'The men walks to the shop', where the verb does not match the subject. This is also true in regional dialects where verb-subject disagreement is a common spoken pattern. Tense is another area where less confident English speakers make mistakes, as they grapple with the complexity of English verb structure. Practice, both oral and written, is paramount.

Linked Speaking and Listening and Writing activities

This section will give you the opportunity to target relevant Speaking and Listening and Writing standards through activities such as those that follow.

Speaking and Listening

- Create a bank of key regional turns of phrase that are common in informal spoken English, but incorrect in formal spoken English or written English, e.g. 'You was five minutes late'. Students could record a short discussion of a topic, television programme or current event, and then listen for phrases that should not be imported into written English *(SLlr/L1.5)*.

Writing

- Revise a piece of informal language, using colloquial terms, into more formal language, or rewrite a passage of writing with a formal register *(Wt/L1.6)*.
- Use a card-sort approach to match 20 singular or plural nouns with the correct verb form *(Ws/L1.2)*.
- Transfer a short passage of writing in one tense into another tense, for example, a radio transcript of a key moment in a football match into a newspaper account of the same moment, requiring a shift from present to past tense *(Ws/L1.2)*.

Photocopiable worksheets

The following photocopiable sheets are included for Section F:

F1 Subject-verb agreement 1

F2 Subject-verb agreement 2

F3 Changing to past tense

F4 *To be* and *to have*

F5 Using *to be* and *to have*

F6 Using the right tense.

F1 Subject-verb agreement 1

This worksheet accompanies **p.72–73** in the *Level 1 Skills Book*

Name ______________________ Date __________

Writers sometimes make mistakes matching the singular and plural of nouns and pronouns with the right verbs.

Singular noun	Singular pronoun	Plural noun	Plural pronoun
table	it	tables	they
dog	it	dogs	they
boyfriend	he	boyfriends	they
lady	she	ladies	they
plant	it	plants	they
girl	she	girls	they
man	he	men	they
	you		you
	I		we

1 Check whether the pronouns and nouns have the right verb to go with them in the table below. Tick the ones that are correct, and put a cross next to the ones that are incorrect. The first one has been done for you.

2 Write the correct version of the verb next to the incorrect one. Keep all the verbs in the present tense.

he go ✗ *he goes*	the dog bark	I am
I has	you walks	I run
you has	they has	they goes
the dogs bark	the child play	the children plays
the girl walks	we am	you have
they is	I have	we are
the man go	we has	you walk
I are	they runs	the man walk

Literacy Teacher's Handbook Level 1 © Edexcel Limited 2006

F2 Subject-verb agreement

This worksheet accompanies **p.72–73** in the *Level 1 Skills Book*

Name ______________________ Date ____________

In this text, the writer has used the wrong verbs to go with the nouns and pronouns. Sometimes the writer has used the wrong tense.

1 Find the mistakes and underline them. The first one has been done for you.

2 Write the correct version above the mistakes. You should be able to find 19 errors.

Capoeira is a Brazilian martial art developed originally by African slaves who had been brought to Brazil to farms [*farm*] the plantations in Brazil. Many of the slaves come from the west coast of Africa, where they practised martial arts, but when they was brought to Brazil, they is not able to practise their martial arts because it were banned by the plantation owners who see it as a threat.

Capoeira are performed with a partner and there is songs and music that accompany the movements. Some of the songs and music is very slow. This are called 'Angola', whereas 'Regional' music and songs is much faster in tempo. Capoeiristas, which are the name for people who practise capoeira, performs moves with their partner. This are called the 'ginga' where you practises your skill. There is different types of move which falls into the following categories: attack, defence, combinations and acrobatics. Action films and computer games has made capoeira popular. Lots of computer fighting games have characters who uses capoeira as their style of choice.

F3 Changing to past tense

This worksheet accompanies **p.70–71** in the *Level 1 Skills Book*

Name ______________________ Date __________

1 Read the following transcript of a football match. Underline any verbs that are written in the present tense.

2 Then change these verbs to put the transcript into past tense, writing the new verb above the old one. The first one has been done for you.

It was

Commentator 1: It's just after half time. Lewis is restarting the match, along with his fellow midfielder, Sean Atherton. They both came on loan from Hampton Athletic and they've turned out to be real bargains. Atherton's scored five times this season from set pieces, and with Lewis alongside him, they make quite a team. Newtown have a fight on their hands coming back on to the pitch one-nil down, but their manager said he had faith they can come back from this. His half time talk must have put some fire in their souls, because here comes Newtown's John Peters, straight out of nowhere. What a start!

Commentator 2: And off he goes! That was a good pass from Lewis – straight to Peters' feet. Barton FC don't have a chance! Peters seems to have caught the Barton defenders half asleep! Their number two, Pilkington, seems to have woken up now – here he comes with a tackle – oh, he's late! Here comes a free kick, that's for sure! And the ref's blowing his whistle. Yes, it's a free kick to Newtown, right on the edge of the penalty box. Peters must wish he'd made a few more strides. It would have been a penalty! Atherton's coming up to take the free kick. Barton have three men in the wall and their goalie, Latham, he is trying to get them in position, but it is a bit of a shambles really. Atherton has Lewis just to his left. Surely he is going to chip it over. And he does. Goal! One-one!

Literacy Teacher's Handbook Level 1 © Edexcel Limited 2006

F4 *To be and to have*

This worksheet accompanies **p.70–73** in the *Level 1 Skills Book*

Name ________________________ Date __________

Read the table below about *to be* and *to have*. Mistakes in the use of these verbs are very common in writing.

To be (present tense)	To be (past tense)	To have (present tense)	To have (past tense)
I *am*	I *was*	I *have*	I *had*
you *are*	you *were*	you *have*	you *had*
he/she/it *is*	he/she/it *was*	he/she/it *has*	he/she/it *had*
we *are*	we *were*	we *have*	we *had*
you *are*	you *were*	you *have*	you *had*
they *are*	they *were*	they *have*	they *had*

Now fill in the blanks in the text below by adding the correct version of the verb *to be* or *to have* from the table.

I __________ really into martial arts. I __________ a black belt in judo by the age of 17, and it __________ my ambition to get a black belt in three other martial arts by the time I __________ 30. My judo teacher __________ also a ju-jitsu teacher, so he suggested I take up ju-jitsu because it __________ similar in some ways to judo. I __________ now a black belt in ju-jitsu as well and I __________ awarded my belt in Kyoto during a competition. It __________ the proudest moment of my life!

I also do capoeira, which __________ a non-contact martial art, although it looks a bit like a dance. You __________ partnered up and you work as a partnership to practise attacks and blocks. It __________ hard because you __________ to know when your partner __________ going to make an attacking move, and you __________ to decide whether to make a counter-attack, mirror their attack, block it or do an acrobatic move to get out of the attack.

F5 Using *to be* and *to have*

This worksheet accompanies **p.70–73** in the *Level 1 Skills Book*

Name ______________________________ Date ______________

To be and *to have* are the most commonly used verbs in the English language, so it is not surprising that more mistakes are made with these verbs than with others.

1 Look at the verb phrases in the table and write them in where they need to go on the time line. For example, *I had* is past tense and *I will have* refers to an action in the future.

Past	Present	Future
I had		*I will have*

I had	I was	I have
they were	they had	they will have
they have	I will be	I am
I will have	they are	they will be

2 Use the phrases from the box above to fill the gaps below.

A Last year ______________ a job so that I could earn some extra money.

B When they gave me the job ______________ a shortage of staff.

C After six months I gave up the job because ______________ too busy.

D They said that in the future ______________ happy to give me another job.

E In the holidays I will have more time so ______________ able to work there again.

F I was very happy working there so I think ______________ very good employers.

Literacy Teacher's Handbook Level 1 © Edexcel Limited 2006

F6 Using the right tense

This worksheet accompanies **p.70–71** in the *Level 1 Skills Book*

Name ______________________ Date __________

Sometimes writers change tense while writing. This can be done for effect, or to show a contrast between how things were, how they developed and how they are now.

- Verbs in the **present** tense refer to things that are happening now, e.g. *It is raining. I am wet. We are getting soaked!*
- Verbs in the **future** tense refer to things that will happen in the future, e.g. *David will meet us there. The match is going to be cancelled.*
- Verbs in the **past** tense refer to things that have already happened, e.g. *My dog ate the cake. He was standing with his paws on the table.*

1 Read the text below and underline the verbs. Write **past**, **present** or **future** above each verb. The first one has been done for you.

> *present*
>
> There is a huge range of martial arts across the world. Although martial arts started in East Asian countries many centuries ago, new martial arts are still being developed in countries as far apart as Japan and Brazil. Some martial arts use nothing but hand-to-hand combat techniques, like kicks, punches and throws, whereas other martial arts include weaponry as well, like sword fighting (such as kendo) or stick fighting (such as bojitsu or jojitsu). Martial arts began to be popular in the West during the 1950s, and now many people across the whole world enjoy taking part. It is predicted that martial arts will continue to grow in popularity and more and more people will become involved.

2 Write the correct verbs to fill the gaps in these sentences. Make sure you use the correct tense.

A I wanted to speak to Chris so I __________ him on his mobile.

B Chris __________ going on holiday tomorrow.

C I __________ to talk to him today.

G Preparing for the test

(pages 76–93 in the Skills Book)

This section of the Teacher's Handbook contains a range of photocopiable sheets for students to use, including:

- advice about how to prepare for the test
- guidance on how to achieve optimum performance in the test
- a practice test with answers
- answers to the worksheets in other sections
- additional worksheets to help students revise question types that they find difficult.

Each part of this section has been designed so that it can be photocopied for students.

G1 Top tips for the test

This section gives advice about how to prepare for the test, and how to approach the test on the day.

G2 How to tackle different kinds of question

This section gives examples of many of the question types that students are likely to face in the test. Explanations clarify what each question is asking.

G3 Test vocabulary

This section contains typical test questions and explains any technical vocabulary that may give students problems.

G4 Test

Section G4 presents six test questions on each of four passages. These cover the main types of question that the students are likely to encounter in the test.

G5 Test answers

Answers are provided for the tests in Sections G2 and G4. For each question the students are directed to similar question types that appear in worksheets in Section G6. In this way students are given further practice on question types that they have found difficult.

G6 Worksheets

Three additional worksheets are provided so that students can have even more test practice. These worksheets directly support the tests in Sections G2 and G4. Answers are provided in Section G5.

Answers to worksheets

Answers are provided for the worksheets in Sections A to F.

G1 Top tips for the test

Preparing for the test

- Look back at what you have been taught and revise everything thoroughly. Go back over any sections of the Skills Book that you found difficult, and do the practice tests in sections G4 and G6. Use the Hot Topics CD-Rom to help you revise grammar and punctuation.
- Sections G2 and G3 (pages 76–78) of the Teacher's Handbook will help you revise the main question types and vocabulary that you may meet in the test.
- Do the tests on the Practice Tests CD-Rom, and time yourself. This will help you:
  - understand how the paper is set out
  - recognise the different types of questions
  - find out how fast you have to work
  - see if there is anything you need to learn again.
- Revise with a friend, testing each other on aspects of the test specification and discussing each other's answers.
- Start your revision early so that you have time to talk to your tutor and get help with any problems you may have.

On the day of the test

- Make sure that you have everything you need and leave behind things that are not allowed, such as your mobile phone and calculator.
- Listen carefully to what the invigilator has to say, and then read the instructions for the test carefully.
- Remember, for each question you must always choose only ONE answer from the four choices that you are given. Read all four carefully before making your choice.
- If you do not know an answer, try to work it out rather than guess. If you are unsure of your answer, mark it for review at the end of the test. No points are deducted for wrong answers so don't leave any blanks.
- Time your progress. Make sure that you have enough time to answer all the questions and leave a few minutes for checking. If you are taking the test on screen, you will be able to see how much time is remaining throughout the test. It is important to pace yourself.
- When you come to the end, check your answers for any mistakes before finishing the test.

G2 How to tackle different kinds of question (1)

Name ______________________ Date __________

> **Remember**
> - sometimes all the possible answers may look as if they answer the question – then you have to think hard about which is the best answer
> - even if several answers look right, only one answer is correct and you need to identify it.

All of the questions in the test are multiple-choice. You will be given four possible answers and you will have to choose the ONE correct answer. You need to:

- read each question very carefully so that you are sure what it is asking you
- read all of the possible answers and choose the option that best answers the question.

Think about the different kinds of question you'll be asked in the test. You need to identify which skills each question requires you to use.

Read the sample questions below and tick the answer that best describes what you would need to do in order to answer the question. In this activity you do not need to answer the actual question, but think about *how* you would find the answer. The first one has been done for you.

How would you tackle these types of question?

1 In which year did Jimi Hendrix die?

A Skim the text to work out what it's about. ☐

B Scan the text to find the right date. ☑

C Read the text carefully from beginning to end. ☐

2 What is the main point in the first paragraph?

A Read the text carefully from beginning to end. ☐

B Scan the whole text to find key words. ☐

C Find the first paragraph and skim to work out what it's about, then read it carefully to check you've found the main point. ☐

3 Which of the following would be the best heading for this document?

A Skim the whole text to work out what it's about. ☐

B Read the text carefully from beginning to end. ☐

C Scan the text to find a key word. ☐

4 What is the purpose of this document?

A Read the text carefully from beginning to end. ☐

B Scan the whole text to find key words. ☐

C Skim the text to work out what it's about and who it is for, then read it carefully to check this against the possible answers. ☐

Literacy Teacher's Handbook Level 1 © Edexcel Limited 2006

G2 How to tackle different kinds of question (2)

Name ______________________ Date __________

5 The best word to replace 'represented' on line 9 would be

A Read the whole text carefully from beginning to end. ☐

B Read the paragraph containing 'represented' and think about what the word means, then try out all the suggested words in the sentence and see which works best. ☐

C Look at the suggested words and see which of them means the same as 'represented'. ☐

6 Which of these phrases in lines 7–9 contains a word that's used incorrectly?

A Read lines 7–9 and look out for any words that look wrong. ☐

B Scan the whole document to find words that are used incorrectly. ☐

C Read lines 7–9 and then read the phrases listed in the answers; look out for a word in these phrases that has been used incorrectly (often a word that sounds the same as another word but is spelled differently). ☐

7 On which of the following lines did the writer make a grammatical error?

A Read the whole text carefully, looking out for grammatical errors. ☐

B Read the lines in the suggested answers and look out for wrong use of tenses or places where the subject and verb of a sentence don't agree. ☐

C Scan the text, looking out for grammatical errors. ☐

8 On which of the following lines is there an incomplete sentence?

A Read each of the lines mentioned and look for sentences that do not contain a verb or that do not end with a full stop, question mark or exclamation mark. ☐

B Scan the whole text, looking for sentences that do not contain a verb or that do not end with a full stop, question mark or exclamation mark. ☐

C Read the whole text carefully, looking out for incomplete sentences. ☐

9 Which of the following punctuation marks is missing on line 11?

A Read the whole text carefully, looking out for missing punctuation marks. ☐

B Read line 11 and look out for missing punctuation marks. ☐

C Read the whole paragraph around line 11 and work out what it means, then check the list of missing punctuation marks and work out which of them is missing on line 11. ☐

10 On which of the following lines should the writer have begun a new paragraph?

A Read the whole text carefully, looking out for places where a new paragraph could start. ☐

B Read the lines mentioned in the answers and choose the one that looks like the best place for a paragraph to start. ☐

C Skim the whole text and get a sense of the main points covered in each paragraph; then look at the suggested answers and choose the answer that shows a line where a new main point is introduced. ☐

G3 Test vocabulary

In the test you will meet vocabulary that is used very specifically and you will need to know exactly what this vocabulary means in order to answer the questions accurately. Below are some of the words you are most likely to meet in questions, with explanations of what these questions are asking you to do.

1 What is the best word or phrase to **replace** 'expire' on line 4?

A die ☐

B run out of time ☐

C become invalid ☐

D disappear. ☐

This question is asking **what word or phrase (group of words) means the same as** 'expire'. Be careful – sometimes words have more than one meaning. You need to find the word or phrase that means the same as this word in this passage.

2 What is the **grammatical error** on line 8?

Grammatical errors can mean things like mistakes with tenses (e.g. 'Yesterday I will go') or mistakes with verb-subject agreement (e.g. 'We was going to the supermarket').

3 Which phrase does not suit the **formal tone** of this extract?

You would expect a **formal tone** in a textbook or official letter: complete sentences, Standard English, technical words. You would expect an **informal tone** in a note or an e-mail to a friend: abbreviations, slang, incomplete sentences, simple words.

4 In this **draft document** there are a number of spelling errors.

When you write something and then check it carefully before writing out a final copy, the first version is a **draft**. When the word 'draft' is used in the test, it often indicates that there are mistakes in the document.

5 Which **statement** best describes the way the writer of this document feels about recycling?

In the test, a **statement** is a sentence or a phrase that sums something up – e.g. 'She is in favour of recycling' or 'She feels recycling is unnecessary'.

6 What is the **purpose** of this document?

A To inform and explain ☐

B To entertain ☐

C To persuade the reader ☐

D To describe the scene ☐

The **purpose** of a document is the reason it was written. You can normally tell the purpose by looking at the features of the document, and by thinking about the message it is trying to give to the reader.

7 What **punctuation** error has been made on line 3?

Questions about punctuation are usually asking you to notice where a **full stop**, **question mark**, **comma** or **apostrophe** has been used wrongly or left out.

8 What is the writer's **main aim** in this extract?

The writer's main aim is what they **most** want to achieve in their writing. They may have more than one aim (e.g. to inform and entertain) so you need to think about which aim is most important.

G4 Test 1

Name ______________________ Date __________

Questions 1–6 are based on the document below.

In a peat bog near Llanwrtyd Wells in Wales, a strange sporting event takes place each August Bank Holiday – the World Bog Snorkelling Championship.

To take part, competitors have to swim up and down a trench cut into the peat bog. The trench is over 50 metres long and full of dirty, smelly, muddy water. Competitors have to wear snorkels and flippers (wetsuits are optional). They are not allowed to use any 'proper' swimming strokes – only doggy paddle. The first prize is just £40.

So why would anyone want to do this Well – it's fun! Competitors come from all over the world, and some people take it more seriously than others. In 2006, one competitor wore a pyjama suit with Australian emblems – and so did his dog! 2006 was the 21st anniversary of the __________, and for the first time ever there was a tie for first place – resulting in a rematch or 'bog off', between competitors Haydn Pitchford and Glenn Marshall. In the end, Haydn Pitchford won by just one second!

1 According to the text, how long has the World Bog Snorkelling Championship been running?

- **A** ☐ 21 years
- **B** ☐ 50 years
- **C** ☐ 40 years
- **D** ☐ 2 years

2 What is the main purpose of the text?

- **A** ☐ To tell readers who won the World Bog Snorkelling Championship in 2006
- **B** ☐ To describe the World Bog Snorkelling Championship
- **C** ☐ To persuade readers to take part in the Championship
- **D** ☐ To give information about the history of bog snorkelling

3 What is the main point in paragraph 3?

- **A** ☐ The World Bog Snorkelling Championship is fun
- **B** ☐ The Championship is a tough event to compete in
- **C** ☐ It's strange that anyone wants to take part in the Championship
- **D** ☐ Competitors come from all over the world

4 According to the text, what equipment do you need to take part in the World Bog Snorkelling Championship?

- **A** ☐ Snorkel, flippers and wetsuit
- **B** ☐ Snorkel and wetsuit
- **C** ☐ Snorkel and flippers
- **D** ☐ Snorkel, flippers and pyjamas

5 What is the correct spelling of the word missing from line 10?

- **A** ☐ compettition
- **B** ☐ competishion
- **C** ☐ compatition
- **D** ☐ competition

6 What punctuation mark is missing on line 7?

- **A** ☐ full stop
- **B** ☐ comma
- **C** ☐ question mark
- **D** ☐ apostrophe

G4 Test 2

Name ______________________________ Date ____________

Questions 7–12 are based on the following draft document.

> **Sign our petition and SHOUT OUT for affordable housing!**
>
> Did you know that the Council is about to consider proposals to build new houses on the edge of town? The idea is that these houses would be priced, cheaply enough so that local people can afford to by them.
>
> Some people don't like this idea – they say that their is no room in town for more houses, or that the houses will be an eyesore. But we say that this new housing __________ is ESSENTIAL. At the moment, house prices locally are so high that young people can't even afford to rent, let alone buy a house. Lots of houses are being bought by wealthy people who want to use them as holiday homes, forcing out local people. Sign our petition today and help get the message across to the Council.

7 What is the main purpose of this text?

- **A** ☐ To persuade readers that the proposal to build new houses on the edge of town is a bad idea because there isn't room
- **B** ☐ To explain why young people cannot afford to buy houses locally
- **C** ☐ To persuade readers to sign a petition in support of affordable housing
- **D** ☐ To explain the Council's plans with regard to affordable housing

8 What is the correct spelling of the word missing on line 8?

- **A** ☐ developement
- **B** ☐ develepment
- **C** ☐ developemant
- **D** ☐ development

9 On what line has a word been used incorrectly?

- **A** ☐ line 2
- **B** ☐ line 4
- **C** ☐ line 6
- **D** ☐ line 9

10 What is the main point in paragraph 2 (lines 6–13)?

- **A** ☐ The petition is a good way of getting a message to the Council.
- **B** ☐ The new housing development is a bad idea.
- **C** ☐ The new housing development is a good idea.
- **D** ☐ Wealthy people should not be allowed to buy houses locally.

11 On which of the following lines should the writer have started a new paragraph?

- **A** ☐ line 3
- **B** ☐ line 7
- **C** ☐ line 9
- **D** ☐ line 12

12 On which line has a comma been misused?

- **A** ☐ line 4
- **B** ☐ line 7
- **C** ☐ line 10
- **D** ☐ line 12

Literacy Teacher's Handbook Level 1 © Edexcel Limited 2006

G4 Test 3

Name ____________________ Date __________

Questions 13–18 are based on the document below.

Welcome to Birchmere Swimming Pool!
We are open 7 a.m.–9 p.m. Monday to Friday, and 9 a.m.–9 p.m. Saturday and Sunday.
Open swimming sessions are on Weekday mornings 9–11 a.m., and at weekends 10 a.m.–2 p.m.
In addition, we offer the following special activities.

Day	Adult lane swimming	Parent and toddler	Disabled swim session	Women only session	Family fun (slides and inflatables)	Aquacise (exercise in water)
Monday	7–9 a.m.			8–9 p.m.		
Tuesday	7–9 a.m.		3–4 p.m.			11–12 a.m.
Wednesday	7–9 a.m.	11–12 a.m.		8–9 p.m.		
Thursday	7–9 a.m.		6.30–7.30 p.m.			8–9 p.m.
Friday	7–9 a.m.	1–2 p.m.		8–9 p.m.		
Saturday	7–8 p.m.		9–10 a.m.		2–5 p.m.	
Sunday	7–8 p.m.				2–5 p.m.	8–9 p.m.

13 Where is this document most likely to have come from?

- **A** ☐ a newspaper advertisement
- **B** ☐ a letter
- **C** ☐ a leaflet
- **D** ☐ a guidebook for tourists

14 According to the table, when could swimmers take part in an Aquacise session?

- **A** ☐ Mondays 7–9 a.m.
- **B** ☐ Tuesdays 11–12 a.m.
- **C** ☐ Wednesdays 11–12 a.m.
- **D** ☐ Fridays 8–9 p.m.

15 If you just wanted to swim, rather than take part in a special activity, when should you come to the pool?

- **A** ☐ Weekday mornings 9–11 a.m.
- **B** ☐ Weekends 10 a.m.–2 p.m.
- **C** ☐ Thursday and Friday afternoons
- **D** ☐ Weekday mornings 9–11 a.m. and weekends 10 a.m.–2 p.m.

16 On which days are there special swimming sessions for disabled people?

- **A** ☐ Tuesday and Saturday
- **B** ☐ Monday, Thursday and Saturday
- **C** ☐ Tuesday, Thursday and Saturday
- **D** ☐ Tuesday, Thursday and Sunday

17 Which of the following statements is true, according to the chart?

- **A** ☐ The pool is open every day 7 a.m.–9 p.m.
- **B** ☐ Aquacise sessions only run on weekdays.
- **C** ☐ The only adult lane swimming sessions are early in the morning.
- **D** ☐ Family fun sessions only run at the weekend.

18 Which of the following words shows an incorrect use of a capital letter?

- **A** ☐ Pool (line 1)
- **B** ☐ Sunday (line 2)
- **C** ☐ Open (line 3)
- **D** ☐ Weekday (line 3)

G4 Test 4

Name ______________________ Date ____________

Questions 19–24 are based on the draft letter below.

Dear Sir or Madam,

I wish to complain about a problem with a packet of Munch Brothers' Amazing Chocolate Strawberry Flapjacks, which I bought on saturday 24 April.

When I open the packet, imagine my horror when I saw a large green beetle stuck to the top biscuit. I was going to offer the biscuit to my son, aged 3. Their were a similar large green beetle stuck to another biscuit too. Needless to say, I threw both biscuits __________ in the bin.

I am enclosing the rest of the packet with this letter and I look forward to __________ both an apology and a refund.

Love,

Mrs Janet Butcher

19 What is the correct spelling of the missing word on line 11?

- **A** ☐ recieving
- **B** ☐ reseiving
- **C** ☐ receiving
- **D** ☐ recceiving

20 On which line is there a capital letter missing?

- **A** ☐ line 2
- **B** ☐ line 4
- **C** ☐ line 7
- **D** ☐ line 11

21 On which lines are there grammatical errors?

- **A** ☐ lines 5 and 8
- **B** ☐ lines 3 and 7
- **C** ☐ lines 5 and 7
- **D** ☐ lines 3 and 8

22 On which line has a word been misused?

- **A** ☐ line 2
- **B** ☐ line 3
- **C** ☐ line 4
- **D** ☐ line 7

23 The correct spelling of the missing word on line 9 is

- **A** ☐ strait
- **B** ☐ straiht
- **C** ☐ straght
- **D** ☐ straight

24 Which line contains a word that is too informal for this letter?

- **A** ☐ line 2
- **B** ☐ line 4
- **C** ☐ line 6
- **D** ☐ line 12

Literacy Teacher's Handbook Level 1 © Edexcel Limited 2006

G4 Test 5

Name ____________________ Date __________

Questions 25–30 are based on the document below.

Have you ever wondered how the bubbles get into a loaf of bread. If you look carefully at a slice of bread, you will see that their are lots of small bubbles and holes. These are caused by the yeast which bakers add to flour and liquid when they are making bread.

Yeast is amazing! It is a sort of fungus, but it can be dried out and turned into a powder which can be kept for months. Yeast is not only used in bread-making – it also goes into wine and beer.

If you add warm water to yeast, you will see it begin to froth and bubble up. If you add flour to the bubbling yeast mixture you can make a bread dough, the yeast in the dough will begin to feed on the flour and start growing and multiplying. As the yeast grows it gives off a gas called carbon dioxide. This gas bubbles up through the dough and makes it rise up and turn puffy. This is how the bubbles of air get into a loaf of bread.

25 What is the main purpose of this document?

- **A** ☐ To persuade the reader to use yeast when making bread
- **B** ☐ To explain how yeast makes the bubbles in bread
- **C** ☐ To describe how bread is made
- **D** ☐ To give instructions for making bread

26 On which line is there a missing question mark?

- **A** ☐ line 2
- **B** ☐ line 3
- **C** ☐ line 9
- **D** ☐ line 17

27 On which line has a word been misused?

- **A** ☐ line 1
- **B** ☐ line 2
- **C** ☐ line 3
- **D** ☐ line 8

28 The most suitable heading for paragraph 3 would be:

- **A** ☐ How to make a bread dough
- **B** ☐ Baking bread
- **C** ☐ Yeast and carbon dioxide
- **D** ☐ How yeast works

29 On which line has a comma been misused?

- **A** ☐ line 2
- **B** ☐ line 6
- **C** ☐ line 10
- **D** ☐ line 12

30 Which of the following is **not** true of yeast according to the text?

- **A** ☐ It is a type of fungus.
- **B** ☐ It is used in making beer.
- **C** ☐ It is made from flour and water.
- **D** ☐ It produces carbon dioxide.

G5 Answers: Teacher's Handbook practice tests G2 and G4

The two tables below give the answers to G2 and G4. They also tell you what type of question each of the questions is. If there are any question types that you find difficult, check the table on page 85 to find more questions of that type so that you can practise them.

G2 Answers

This is the answer. Tick the box if you got it correct	This is the skill that this question was testing
1B ☐	Scanning
2C ☐	Skimming and close reading
3A ☐	Skimming
4C ☐	Skimming and close reading
5B ☐	Working out what a word means
6C ☐	Spotting misused words
7B ☐	Spotting grammatical errors
8A ☐	Spotting grammatical errors
9C ☐	Spotting punctuation errors
10C ☐	Paragraphing

G4 Answers

This is the answer. Tick the box if you got it correct	This is the skill that this question was testing
1A ☐	Scanning to find detail
2B ☐	Skimming and close reading to identify purpose
3A ☐	Skimming and close reading to identify main point
4C ☐	Scanning and close reading to find detail
5D ☐	Spelling
6C ☐	Spotting punctuation errors
7C ☐	Skimming and close reading to identify purpose
8D ☐	Spelling
9B ☐	Spotting misused words
10C ☐	Skimming and close reading to identify main point
11D ☐	Paragraphing
12A ☐	Spotting punctuation errors
13C ☐	Skimming to identify source
14B ☐	Close reading for detail
15D ☐	Close reading for detail

This is the answer. Tick the box if you got it correct	This is the skill that this question was testing
16C ☐	Close reading for detail
17D ☐	Close reading for detail
18D ☐	Spotting errors in using capital letters
19C ☐	Spelling
20B ☐	Spotting errors in using capital letters
21B ☐	Spotting grammatical errors
22D ☐	Spotting misused words
23D ☐	Spelling
24D ☐	Spotting formal/informal tone
25B ☐	Skimming and close reading to identify purpose
26A ☐	Spotting punctuation errors
27B ☐	Spotting misused words
28D ☐	Close reading to identify main point
29D ☐	Spotting punctuation errors
30C ☐	Close reading for detail

Literacy Teacher's Handbook Level 1 © Edexcel Limited 2006

G6 worksheets and answers

Once you have completed G2 and G4 and checked your answers, look at the table on page 84 to find out if there are any skills you need to practise more. Find those skills in the table below and then look in the right-hand columns to find more questions of this type to give you further practice. The answers to these questions are in the tables at the bottom of the page.

Where to find questions of a similar type in the G6 worksheets

Question type	Where to find more examples in G6	
	Worksheet	**Question number**
Scanning and close reading to find detail	G6 Test 2	1
Skimming and close reading to work out purpose	G6 Test 1	1
Skimming and close reading to work out main point	G6 Test 1	5
Skimming to identify source	G6 Test 3	1
Working out what a word means	G6 Test 2	3
Spotting misused words	G6 Test 3	5
Spotting grammatical errors	G6 Test 1 G6 Test 2	3 5
Spotting punctuation errors	G6 Test 3	4
Spotting errors in using capital letters	G6 Test 3	4
Spotting formal/informal tone	G6 Test 2	2
Paragraphing	G6 Test 3	3
Spelling	G6 Test 1 G6 Test 3	2 2

Answers to G6 worksheets

Worksheet G6A	Worksheet G6B	Worksheet G6C
1B ☐	1A ☐	1D ☐
2A ☐	2C ☐	2B ☐
3D ☐	3D ☐	3B ☐
4C ☐	4B ☐	4B ☐
5B ☐	5C ☐	5D ☐

Answers to Section G of the Skills Book

Answers to Skills Book Section G1

This is the answer. Tick the box if you got it correct	This is the skill that this question was testing
1A ☐	Scanning and close reading to find detail
2B ☐	Scanning and close reading to find detail
3B ☐	Close reading for detail
4C ☐	Skimming and close reading to identify main point
5A ☐	Skimming and close reading to identify purpose
6B ☐	Close reading for detail
7D ☐	Close reading for detail

Answers to Skills Book Section G2

This is the answer. Tick the box if you got it correct	This is the skill that this question was testing
1C ☐	Skimming and close reading to identify purpose
2C ☐	Scanning and close reading to find detail
3C ☐	Skimming and close reading to identify main point
4C ☐	Close reading for detail
5D ☐	Scanning and close reading to find detail
6C ☐	Close reading for detail
7B ☐	Skimming and close reading to identify main point
8C ☐	Close reading for detail

Answers to Skills Book Section G3

This is the answer. Tick the box if you got it correct	This is the skill that this question was testing
1D ☐	Working out what a word means
2D ☐	Spotting misused words
3C ☐	Close reading for detail
4A ☐	Close reading for detail
5A ☐	Spotting grammatical errors
6D ☐	Spotting grammatical errors
7D ☐	Spotting errors in using capital letters
8C ☐	Spotting errors in using capital letters
9B ☐	Spotting punctuation errors
10C ☐	Paragraphing
11C ☐	Spotting punctuation errors
12A ☐	Spotting punctuation errors
13A ☐	Spelling
14D ☐	Spelling
15C ☐	Spelling
16A ☐	Spelling
17B ☐	Spelling
18C ☐	Spelling

Literacy Teacher's Handbook Level 1 © Edexcel Limited 2006

G6 Worksheet A

Name ______________________________ Date __________

Questions 1–5 are based on the text below.

Leicester is the tenth largest city in the UK, with a population of 280,000. People have lived in Leicester since the time of the Romans, and there are still some interesting remains of Roman buildings – including the famous Jewry wall which has stood for over 2000 years.

Nowadays, Leicester is a successful commercial and manufacturing centre, with a very varied range of __________ and industries. Leicester is also a truly multicultural city, with a third of Leicester's population coming from the thriving ethnic minority Community. The multicultural mix helps ensure that Leicester was an enjoyable and exciting place to live, with events such as the city-wide annual Diwali celebrations and the extremely popular Caribbean Carnival during the summer.

1 What is the main purpose of this text?

A ☐ To persuade readers to visit Leicester
B ☐ To describe what Leicester is like
C ☐ To explain Leicester's history
D ☐ To explain why Leicester is a multicultural city

2 What is the correct spelling of the missing word on line 7?

A ☐ businesses
B ☐ busynesses
C ☐ busineses
D ☐ bussinesses

3 On which line has the wrong tense been used?

A ☐ line 1
B ☐ line 2
C ☐ line 4
D ☐ line 10

4 On which line has a capital letter been used wrongly?

A ☐ line 2
B ☐ line 3
C ☐ line 10
D ☐ line 12

5 Which of the following would be the best heading to use before line 6?

A ☐ Leicester – a successful manufacturing centre
B ☐ Leicester today
C ☐ Celebrate Diwali in Leicester
D ☐ Multicultural events in Leicester

G6 Worksheet B

Name ______________________ Date __________

Questions 1–5 are based on the newspaper article below.

Fifteen-year-old Justine Somper was hailed a heroine yesterday for saving the life of a complete stranger. Justine was walking her dog through Gates Park in doncaster when she heard a splash. In front of her 8-year-old Sonya Hartnett slipped into the boating lake and disappeared under the surface. Without thinking about her own safety Justine jumped in, felt frantically under the surface and fished Sonya's limp body out of the water. __________ a passing fire-fighter, Ian James, 40, was on hand to give Sonya the kiss of life. L8R Sonya was taken to hospital where she is expected to make a full recovery.

Sonya's mother, 31-year-old Joan Hartnett, said Justine's a heroine. She saved my lovely daughter's life and I __________ grateful for the rest of my life. That girl should get a reward."

1 According to the newspaper article which of the following is true?

A ☐ Justine was walking her dog through the park.

B ☐ Sonya was walking her dog through the park.

C ☐ Ian James was walking his dog through the park.

D ☐ Joan Hartnett was walking her dog through the park.

2 Which line contains a word that is too informal for this text?

A ☐ line 3

B ☐ line 5

C ☐ line 9

D ☐ line 12

3 What would be the best word to replace 'frantically' in line 6?

A ☐ cleverly

B ☐ calmly

C ☐ quickly

D ☐ urgently

4 On which line has a capital letter been missed out?

A ☐ line 1

B ☐ line 3

C ☐ line 8

D ☐ line 9

5 What would be the correct verb to use in the gap on line 12?

A ☐ was

B ☐ would be

C ☐ will be

D ☐ were

Literacy Teacher's Handbook Level 1 © Edexcel Limited 2006

G6 Worksheet C

Name ____________________ Date __________

Questions 1–5 are based on the draft text below.

To: Sheila Blunt, Catering Manager

From: Simon Offstone

Date: 13 March 2007

Choice of food on canteen menu

We have received a number of complaints lately about the narrow range of choices available on the canteen menu. For example, last Thursday the only main course options were sausages beans and chips or burger and chips.
We need to make sure there is at least one vegetarian main course, as well as a range of healthier options. I wood like to arrange a meeting with you to discuss menu planning and agree the way forward. Please telephone my secretary to arrange an __________ during the coming week.

1 This text is most likely to have come from

- **A** ☐ a letter
- **B** ☐ a report
- **C** ☐ a poster
- **D** ☐ a memo

2 What is the correct spelling of the missing word in line 13?

- **A** ☐ apointment
- **B** ☐ appointment
- **C** ☐ appontement
- **D** ☐ apointmant

3 On which line could the writer have best begun a new paragraph?

- **A** ☐ line 6
- **B** ☐ line 10
- **C** ☐ line 11
- **D** ☐ line 12

4 On which line is a comma missing?

- **A** ☐ line 6
- **B** ☐ line 7
- **C** ☐ line 9
- **D** ☐ line 12

5 On which line has a word been used in error?

- **A** ☐ line 5
- **B** ☐ line 7
- **C** ☐ line 9
- **D** ☐ line 10

Answers to worksheets

A1: page 26

1 Scanning is reading over a whole text at speed, not reading every word but searching for key words.

Skimming is reading quickly through a text to get an overview of what it is about.

Close reading is reading in detail, focusing in on what you are reading.

2 Highlight words or sentences *sc, c-r*
Look at illustrations and pictures *sk*
Look at longer words that stand out *sc*
Look at the headings and subheadings *sk*
Look at topic sentences in each paragraph *sk*
Look for bold text or italics *sc, c-r*
Look for key words *sc*
Look for numbers *sc, c-r*
Look for pictures or charts *sc*
Read more slowly *c-r*
Read the introduction more carefully *c-r*
Underline important words *sc, c-r*

A2: page 27

Open question – any questions based on content of menu will be fine.

A3: page 28

The Hotel Beau Rivage is situated near the **delightful** *lovely*
shops, tavernas and **numerous** restaurants in Illetas itself, *many*
children), **extensive** gardens and several paved verandahs *large*
is equipped with a range of spa facilities which you are *has*
Guests can **take advantage of** the three restaurants *use*
The rooms are **spacious** and all have a balcony with a *big*
twin rooms, and include tea and coffee-making **facilities** *equipment*

A4: page 29

1 <u>The thing I like most about skateboarding</u>
<u>The history of the skateboard</u>
<u>tricks</u>

2 1 ✓ C Excitement and friends
2 ✓ B History
3 ✓ A Tricks

A5: page 30

Open question – any responses that tally with the test will do.

Literacy Teacher's Handbook Level 1 © Edexcel Limited 2006

A6: page 31

Open question. Any response that uses all features effectively will do.

B1: page 34

Paragraph 2: phrase 'role playing game', subheading e.g. 'Role playing adventure games'

Paragraph 3: phrase 'sports based', subheading e.g. 'Sports games'

Paragraph 4: phrase 'simulation games', subheading e.g. 'Simulation games'

B2: page 35

Paragraph 1 ———— A game for everyone
Paragraph 2 ———— Be a hero for a day
Paragraph 3 ———— Couch potato or Coach Potato?
Paragraph 4 ———— Control a nation or fly a fighter

B3: page 36

2 C A D B

3 *Open question; answers should refer to content of paragraphs and use of words like 'Another' and 'Some'.*

B4: page 37

1 First, come out of the train station through the main exit opposite the Metrolink platform. You should be facing a road with a taxi rank and several bus stops. Urbis information centre is in front of you.

2 Once you are facing Urbis, go left up to the top of the road, and then turn right, so you are walking alongside the museum. You will see the Printworks on your left hand side and The Triangle in front of you.

3 When you get to The Triangle, you will see the giant TV screen on your right, and the Arndale Centre tower on your left. Selfridges is in front of you, with the giant windmills. Go up between the Arndale and Selfridges, following the road towards Marks & Spencer.

4 When you get to Marks & Spencer, turn left, go underneath the Arndale food court, which is overhead, and continue up Market Street. Keep going up here until you get to Debenhams. Then go past Debenhams. Piccadilly bus station should be on your right. Keep going up to the main junction.

5 At the main junction, you will see pedestrian signs pointing to Piccadilly Station. Keep going straight on. You will see Malmaison Hotel on your right. Once you pass Malmaison Hotel, follow the fork in the road up the incline to Piccadilly Station's entrance.

B5: page 38

7+ — Suitable for people over 7 years of age

(spider) — Contains material some people may find frightening

16+ — Suitable for people over 16 years of age

(fist) — Contains acts of violence

@*! — Contains bad language

B6: page 39

Open question.

C1: page 42

Persuasive — £1 a week means a huge amount to an abandoned dog like me. Your gift will help The Dogs' Trust give us all the love and support we need.

Descriptive — The house is a four-bed semi-detached, occupying a position at the end of a large driveway. There is a large, well-maintained garden to the front, and the garden to the rear has spectacular views of the Lake District.

Informative — Swimming is a good activity for all-round cardio-vascular fitness. It exercises your lungs as well as your body.

Instructive — Before you switch the kettle on, fill it with water. Then you will need to press down the switch until it switches itself off or the water boils.

Explanatory — Volcanoes erupt because of movements in the Earth's surface. When pieces of the Earth's surface (known as plates) move, magma from below the surface is forced up along the edge of the plate.

C2: page 43

Open questions.

C3: page 44

3 *Then* you will need to press the switch so that the water boils.

When the kettle is boiling, prepare the cup by placing the tea bag in it.

If you want a weaker cup of tea, remove the teabag *after* a minute.

Finally add milk and sugar as desired and stir.

C4: page 45

2 *Open question. Any appropriate adjectives will do.*

Literacy Teacher's Handbook Level 1 © Edexcel Limited 2006

C5: page 46

Volcanoes are hills or mountains made of lava *which* comes from below the surface of the Earth. When volcanoes erupt, lava and ash build up and *as a result* a cone shaped hill is formed. A great deal of heat is created when a volcano erupts, and *so* some volcanoes give off clouds of ash and gas. Other volcanoes produce red-hot streams of lava *which* run down their sides. Volcanoes can be formed in the sea as well as on land. Undersea volcanoes sometimes grow very high, *so* their tops reach above the sea level, and *as a result* they form islands.

Volcanoes can cause a great deal of damage, *because* the gas and lava they produce can injure and kill people and animals, and destroy crops and buildings. *Therefore*, when people who live near a volcano get warning that it is about to erupt, they often move away *so* they can avoid danger.

C6: page 47

Open question.

D1: page 50

A strate: straight | plait: plate
mayte: mate | caik: cake
lait: late
Mistake pattern: a_e, aigh

B meat: meet | sweats: sweets
kean: keen | seet: seat
meat: meet
Mistake pattern: ee, ea

C nite: night | lite: light
brite: bright | wright: write
whight: white
Mistake pattern: i_e, igh

D releif: relief | seive: sieve
freind: friend | recieved: received
beleived: believed
Mistake pattern: ie, ei

D2: page 51

Open question.

D3: page 52

1 *Circle:* jelly, lady, baby, penny, fly, puppy, city, pony, bully

2 *Circle:* dish, bus, kiss, coach, gas, box, peach, church, fox, lunch, wish, cross

3 Word pairs:

fox – box | bus – gas
dish – wish | lunch – church
coach – peach | table – dribble
dot – cat | kiss – cross

Answers to worksheets

D4: page 53

Open question.

D5: page 54

1 two ———— a number

too ———— also, as well, a lot or very

to ———— part of an action, or shows where someone went

2 I was going *to* the shops *to* get a couple of pints of milk for breakfast the next morning. I went *to* the fridge and picked up *two* pints of milk. Then I thought I might want some juice to go with breakfast, so I picked up a carton of fresh juice *too*.

"Is that all?" asked the shopkeeper when I got *to* the check-out.

"Can I have a bar of chocolate *too*?" I said, then I remembered my sister. "Better make that *two*," I said. I hate it when she pinches mine.

"One for your sister, *too*?" The shopkeeper asked, with a smile.

"You bet," I said, then left the shop *to* go home.

D6: page 55

Open question.

E1: page 58

1 From: Elizabeth

To: Abigail

Did you have fun on Saturday night? I only saw you in the restaurant but then we went to the Pig and Whistle and I don't know where you got to! I loved it in The Fortune Garden – I had sesame crackers, Kung Pao chicken and several cocktails! It was almost like we were back on holiday! I know drinking cocktails isn't a very Chinese, but I didn't think it was an evening for drinking tea!

Love Elizabeth

2 From: Abigail

To: Elizabeth

I had a terrible night! I had a bad day at work and then at the restaurant I ordered Szechuan pork, which must have disagreed with me. I went home with Paul and his wife Clare, who had come to pick him up. She's really nice, by the way. I think we should ask her to come out with us next time we go out. She must get really bored with Paul! Aren't we planning a night out in November?

Love Abigail

E2: page 59

6 Riversway Terrace
Hazelton
Gloucestershire
GL41 7RG

Discount Holidays
Oxford Road
Swindon
Wiltshire
WL2 3EQ

Monday, 21 November

Dear Sir or Madam

I am writing to say how disappointed I am with my recent holiday with Discount Holidays. I expect a full refund for the reasons I will outline below.

Firstly, the room was in a dreadful state when we arrived. The maid had not finished cleaning, and there was dust everywhere, including on the television set. It was filthy and my wife was disgusted. Secondly, the breakfast was not up to my usual standards. There was no tomato served with the English breakfast and I was disappointed by the fried bread and mushrooms. At night, there was a very loud disco that played terrible pop music. I could barely sleep. We expect a full refund.

Yours sincerely

Mr B Booth

E3: page 60

I enjoyed doing History at school. I particularly enjoyed studying the Vikings and the Middle Ages. I wasn't so keen on reading about Victorian England or the Industrial Revolution. I also liked learning languages, and I really enjoyed French, even though the teacher, Mr Cannon, had a very odd French accent. He sounded more Welsh than French to me! I really wish I'd had the chance to do Spanish or Portuguese, but these weren't taught at our school. I liked some bits of maths, but I found algebra the hardest. I preferred shapes and area rather than working out calculations. My worst bit of maths was graph work, because I was really messy at drawing them.

My favourite subject was art. I really liked all the practical work we did, but I also liked looking at other people's artwork. I really like Georgia O'Keeffe, but I also like artists like Monet and Renoir. English was okay. I enjoyed reading *Of Mice And Men* and I thought the film was really good. We also watched the film of *All My Sons* but I didn't enjoy it as much.

E4: page 61

A teenager has been banned from roaming the streets at night. Ashley Whiteside, 17, has been causing disruption around the streets of Hammersham every evening for the last four months ever since he moved to the area and he has been charged with several counts of drunken behaviour because he was seen drinking alcohol in the streets on numerous occasions and riding a motorbike while under the influence so he was charged with drunk and disorderly behaviour earlier today at Hammersham County Court and as a result the judge issued an Anti-Social Behaviour Order banning Ashley from the streets so his mother said, "I am really disappointed in Ashley but I don't know what to do with him and I can't stop him going out on the streets every night because he just laughs at me so I hope this has taught him a lesson so he realises how serious all this is."

Ashley has also been banned from driving for 18 months because he was caught riding his motorbike while under the influence of alcohol (so) he also received a fine and he will have to retake his driver's test when the full period is up (and) he will also need to attend a series of alcohol abuse clinics to get his drinking under control.

E5: page 62

He was acting like a baby. *S*	Crying over spilt milk. *SF*
Alison has blonde hair. *S*	The hair products were on special offer. *S*
The hair products. *SF*	Basil sat down. *S*
Opening the door. *SF*	The door opened. *S*
Free strawberries. *SF*	Get free strawberries worth £1.49 when you buy a pot of cream. *S*
Now on sale. *SF*	Buy it today. *S*
I always recycle my newspapers. *S*	Bottles and jars too. *SF*
When you get to Reading. *SF*	You need to take the M4. *S*
You look really cool. *S*	In that jacket. *SF*

E6: page 63

Open question.

F1: page 66

he go ✗ *he goes*	the dog bark ✗ *the dog barks*	I am ✓
I has ✗ *I have*	you walks ✗ *you walk*	I run ✓
you has ✗ *you have*	they has ✗ *they have*	they goes ✗ *they go*
the dogs bark ✓	the child play ✗ *the child plays*	the children plays ✗ *the children play*
the girl walks ✓	we am ✗ *we are*	you have ✓
they is ✗ *they are*	I have ✓	we are ✓
the man go ✗ *the man goes*	we has ✗ *we have*	you walk ✓
I are ✗ *I am*	they runs ✗ *they run*	the man walk ✗ *the man walks*

F2: page 67

Capoeira is a Brazilian martial art developed originally by African slaves who had been brought to Brazil to <u>farm</u> the plantations in Brazil. Many of the slaves <u>came</u> from the west coast of Africa, where they practised martial arts, but when they <u>were</u> brought to Brazil, they <u>were</u> not able to practise their martial art because it <u>was</u> banned by the plantation owners who <u>saw</u> it as a threat.

Literacy Teacher's Handbook Level 1 © Edexcel Limited 2006

Capoeira is performed with a partner and there are songs and music that accompany the movements. Some of the songs and music are very slow. This is called 'Angola', whereas 'Regional' music and songs are much faster in tempo. Capoeiristas, which is the name for people who practise capoeira, perform moves with their partner. This is called the 'ginga' where you practise your skill. There are different types of move which fall into the following categories: attack, defence, combinations and acrobatics. Action films and computer games have made capoeira popular. Lots of computer fighting games have characters who use capoeira as their style of choice.

F3: page 68

Commentator 1: It was just after half time. Lewis was restarting the match, along with his fellow midfielder, Sean Atherton. They both came on loan from Hampton Athletic and they've turned out to be real bargains. Atherton's scored five times this season from set pieces, and with Lewis alongside him, they made quite a team. Newtown had a fight on their hands coming back on to the pitch one-nil down, but their manager said he had faith they could come back from this. His half time talk must have put some fire in their souls, because here came Newtown's John Peters, straight out of nowhere. What a start!

Commentator 2: And off he went! That was a good pass from Lewis – straight to Peters' feet. Barton FC didn't have a chance! Peters seemed to have caught the Barton defenders half asleep! Their number two, Pilkington, seemed to have woken up now – here he came with a tackle – oh, he was late! Here came a free kick, that was for sure! And the ref was blowing his whistle. Yes, it was a free kick to Newtown, right on the edge of the penalty box. Peters must wish he'd made a few more strides. It would have been a penalty! Atherton was coming up to take the free kick. Barton had three men in the wall and their goalie, Latham, was trying to get them in position, but it was a bit of a shambles really. Atherton had Lewis just to his left. Surely he was going to chip it over. And he did. Goal! One-one!

F4: page 69

I *am* really into martial arts. I *had* a black belt in judo by the age of 17, and it *is* my ambition to get a black belt in three other martial arts by the time I *am* 30. My judo teacher is also a ju-jitsu teacher, so he suggested I take up ju-jitsu because it *is* similar in some ways to judo. I *am* now a black belt in ju-jitsu as well and I *was* awarded my belt in Kyoto during a competition. It *was* the proudest moment of my life!

I also do capoeira, which *is* a non-contact martial art, although it looks a bit like a dance. You *are* partnered up and you work as a partnership to practise attacks and blocks. It *is* hard because you *have* to know when your partner *is* going to make an attacking move, and you *have* to decide whether to make a counter-attack, mirror their attack, block it or do an acrobatic move to get out of the attack.

F5: page 70

I had	I have	I will have
I was	I am	I will be
they had	they have	they will have
they were	they are	they will be

A Last year *I had* a job so that I could earn some extra money.

B When they gave me the job *they had* a shortage of staff.

C After six months I gave up the job because *I was* too busy.

D They said that in the future *they will be* happy to give me another job.

E In the holidays I will have more time so *I will be* able to work there again.

F I was very happy working there so I think *they are* very good employers.

F6: page 73

1 There is (*present*) a huge range of martial arts across the world. Although martial arts started (*past*) in East Asian countries many centuries ago, new martial arts are (*present*) still being developed in countries as far apart as Japan and Brazil. Some martial arts use (*present*) nothing but hand-to-hand combat techniques, like kicks, punches and throws, whereas other martial arts include (*present*) weaponry as well, like sword fighting (such as kendo) or stick fighting (such as bojitsu or jojitsu). Martial arts began (*past*) to be popular in the West during the 1950s, and now many people across the whole world enjoy (*present*) taking part. It is predicted (*present*) that martial arts will continue (*future*) to grow in popularity and more and more people will become (*future*) involved.

2 **A** I wanted to speak to Chris so I called him on his mobile.

B Chris is going on holiday tomorrow.

C I want to talk to him today.

Literacy Teacher's Handbook Level 1 © Edexcel Limited 2006